Queerly Lutheran

Ministry Rooted in Tradition, Scripture and the Confessions

By Megan M. Rohrer

Second Edition

© 2009 Megan M. Rohrer

QUEERLY LUTHERAN
 Ministry Rooted in Tradition, Scripture and the Confessions
By Megan M. Rohrer

Second Edition © 2016

The Chapter entitled Queerly Saved, was originally published in essay
form as "Queer Soteriology" in Stand Boldly: Lutheran Theology Faces
the Postmodern World, Edited by Eric Trozzo, Three Trees Press, 2009

Front Cover: Painting of St. Sebastian by Peter Paul Reuben
Author Photo by Vince Donovan

ISBN: 978-1-365-10526-5

For those who serve(d) in silence. For those who left. For those who hope for change. For seminarians who bear the fullest weight of the churches discriminatory policies.

Queerly Lutheran would not have been possible without the love, support and hard work of: Jen & the Rude Family; Joel Workin; Jeff Johnson; Grady Kase; Mari Irvin; Margaret Moreland; Darlene Audus; Lura Groen; the religion faculty at Augustana College in Sioux Falls, SD; the volunteers & board of the Welcome Ministry, and Extraordinary Lutheran Ministries.

All honor and glory be to God(dess).

All bible quotations are NRSV unless stated.

LW = Luther's Works

Introduction

"The truth is, however, that the oppressed are not 'marginals,' are not people living 'outside' society. They have always been 'inside' – inside the structure which made them 'beings for others.'"

– Paulo Friere[1]

The Good News is that our Lutheran faith, confessions, history and scripture is indeed Good News for gay, lesbian, bisexual, transgender and queer individuals and their allies. Though the contemporary Lutheran church seems to have forgotten, the church's support for gay, lesbian, transgender, bisexual and queer people is older than the current perception that "homosexuality is sinful." We also seem to have forgotten that the current American understanding of families as one mother, one father and several children is much newer than the queer family systems that have existed throughout our history, sacred stories and in our rituals.

Most theological books and studies that talk about queer folk and queer sexuality focus on seven biblical texts that may or may not have anything to say about contemporary queer life. Debate about these seven texts has divided Lutherans and despite years and years of study we are still unable to articulate consistent Lutheran theology, ritual and practices. This book focuses on the deeper Lutheran charisms that move us in our gut. I hope this book will speak truth to your head, open your heart and enable you to talk about queer life, faith and love in a truly Lutheran way.

I know that some may say that I am only trying to justify my own lifestyle and ministry. Yes, I am queer in both my sexuality

[1] Freire, Paulo, Pedagogy of the Oppressed, translated by Ramos, Myra Bergman, Continuum, 1970, 74.

and gender and I am too young to remember the time before the Evangelical Church in America (ELCA), a time before women could be pastors. I did not even know that a gay, lesbian, bisexual or transgender person could not be a pastor. In fact, I really believed it when they told me that Lutherans believed in a priesthood of ALL believers.

As a lifelong Lutheran, I know that there is nothing I can do, say or write that could ever justify my life; I am saved by grace, through my faith in Jesus. On one level, my life could have been much easier if I acted straight, or decided not to be an ordained minister. Yet on a deeper level, as Luther once proclaimed, "here I stand, I can do no other." Thankfully, I am blessed with a God(dess) whose love is so much bigger than my sexuality and gender (Romans 8:38) and I pray that God(dess) will forgive any typos or false theology forever inked in these pages.

Notes About Language: "Queer" and "God(dess)"

The writers of the Gospel intentionally used provocative words that were instruments of fear and hate to transform the society they lived in and to give glory to God(dess). In fact, the Greek word for "Good News" referred to the news of the Caesar. The gospel writers used a propaganda term as the title of the story of Jesus, because they believed that true "Good News" can only come from God(dess). In the shadow of the gospel writers, I hope to use the words "queer"[2] and "God(dess)" for the same purpose.

"Queer" is a provocative word that has been an instrument of fear and hate. Some have argued that queer people are unnatural and outside of the created order and/or the love of God(dess). Yet, our sacred scriptures show us time and again how God(dess) works through, transforms and empowers those who are labeled "queer" in gender, sexuality, race, age, cognitive ability, character, ethnicity, social status, physical ability and stature. In this book I will turn the word "queer" on its head by describing how a queer creation full of queer characters are ultimately transformed by

---

[2] Queer theory is an established movement that seeks to reclaim the word "queer" for purposes of empowerment and solidarity. See: Jagose, Annamarie, Queer Theory: An Introduction, NYU Press, 1997.

a queer Christ, who makes it impossible for anyone to be called "queer" again.

As you read, please remember that it is impossible to tell if the queer themes, symbols, sacred stories and characters are intended by their original authors. Terms like "queer," "homosexual," "gay," transgender" and "lesbian" were created less than a hundred years ago and contemporary sexuality and gender constructions inadequately describe people, societies and sacred stories from other times. In a more perfect world, we would not need to label and divide ourselves. In this fallen world, it is best to let historical and fictional people label themselves. Still, I believe we are called to find and name the queerness of God(dess) and God(dess)'s creation. Lutherans today, just as Jesus used provocation to enable people to see a broader more welcoming God(dess), must be provocative and affirm boldly that unless the Good News is queer, it is not good news at all.

Like the word "queer," you may also be provoked by the word "God(dess)." Our sacred scriptures are written in languages that have gendered endings. At times the Greek and Hebrew attribute male gender to God(dess), other times female attributions. These gender nuances are lost in English translations. While you are reading, try to avoid separating the gender of God(dess) into "God" or "Goddess." The word "God(dess)" intentionally seeks to articulate a queer sex and gender that is both male/female and masculine/feminine that is more consistent with the gender fluidity found in our sacred scriptures and postmodern understandings of the world and speaks to our both/and Lutheran nature.[3]

---

[3] This gender queer nature of God(dess) is most easily recognized in the Genesis 17. Named "El-Shaddai" or more literally a male gendered God(dess) that is "many breasted."

Lutheran True Confessions:
Lutheran Participation in Queer Oppression

"Before God we should acknowledge that we are guilty of all manner of sins, even those of which we are not aware, as we do in the Lord's Prayer."[4]

- The Book of Concord: The Confessions of the Evangelical Lutheran Church

---

[4] Tappert, T. G. (2000, c1959). *The book of concord : The confessions of the evangelical Lutheran church*. Philadelphia: Fortress Press.

Rooted in Misogyny and Patriarchy

☐

Contemporary Lutherans are struggling to hold on to their core beliefs while living in a postmodern world. We are seeking to become truly evangelical, by becoming more welcoming at our communion tables, expanding the languages of our songs and by supporting emerging church communities. Yet, our church has yet to fully examine and untangle herself from the deeply rooted misogyny and patriarchy that permeates our confessions, Luther's writings and our sacred texts. Whenever possible, I will name and reject the misogyny and patriarchy found in our tradition, confessions, Luther's writings, scripture and in some of the work of other queer theologians.

As I joyfully highlight and seek to illuminate the queerness that has always been present in our traditions, confessions and scripture. I have also intentionally decided not to lift up the queer symbols, stories and characters that are so entangled in violence, misogyny and patriarchy that they cease to be liberating. Specifically, I have excluded the many references to anal rape that are inflicted by and upon characters or is perpetuated by God(dess) that are described (blatantly or through symbols) in the Hebrew Bible, because they are examples of abuse, rather than healthy queer relationships and because they perpetuate the patriarchal assumptions of a phallocentric worldview.[5] Throughout this text, I will talk about the ancient and traditional understandings that embrace queer individuals, but each time I will try to affirm the welcome of queer individuals while rejecting the misogynist and patriarchal assumptions that they are often coupled with.

In this chapter, I will take a closer look at the misogyny and patriarchy in Luther's writings and in our sacred texts in order to reveal the ways that the subjugation of women and femininity has directly led to negative assumptions about queer gender and sexuality. Just as many contemporary Lutheran's have rejected the

---

[5] If you are interested in learning more about the imagery of anal rape in the Hebrew Bible, see The Queer Bible Commentary, ed. Guest, Deryn, et al, SCM Press, 2006; and Queer Exegesis of the Hebrew Bible, ed. Stone, Ken, 2001.

misogyny and patriarchy in Luther's writings and our scriptures, I hope Lutherans will also reject the fear and discrimination of queer people that directly comes from our misogynistic and patriarchal thinking.

Luther on Male Effeminacy

> *Men have broad shoulders and narrow hips, and accordingly they possess intelligence. Women have narrow shoulders and broad hips. Women ought to stay at home;☐ the way they were created indicates this, for they have broad hips and a wide fundament to sit upon [keep house and bear and raise children].*
>
> *– Martin Luther[6]*

> *However, eloquence in women shouldn't be praised; it's more fitting for them to lisp and stammer. This is more becoming to them. – Martin Luther[7]*

> *"Dr. Martin [Luther] replied, "Yes, indeed, eunuchs are more ardent than anybody else, for the passion doesn't disappear but only the power. For my part I'd rather have two pair [of testicles] added than one pair cut off." [8]*

Luther and those involved in writing the Lutheran Confessions, believed that women were the weaker sex,[9] a belief they quoted from scripture (1 Peter 3:7).[10] At times in Luther's writing, he almost seems to disdain women. Contemporary society is not too far from Luther's stance. If we think that ordaining pastors and giving women the right to vote has erased this

---

[6] LW54 *: Table Talk Recorded by Veit Deitrich No 55.*

[7] *LW54: Table Talk Recorded by Anthony Lauterbach, No 4081.*

[8] LW54: *Table Talk.*

[9] See also: *The Augsburg confession* (Latin and German version); The Short Preface to the *Small Catechism*; LW2: *Lectures on Genesis: Chapters 6-14;* LW5: *Lectures on Genesis: Chapters 26-30;* LW6: *Lectures on Genesis: Chapters 31-37;* LW12: *Selected Psalms I;* LW27: *Lectures on Galatians;* and LW28: *1 Corinthians 7, 1 Corinthians 15, Lectures on 1 Timothy.* It should also be said that Luther believed that men could not exist without women and that women ruled over men.

[10] LW5 *: Lectures on Genesis: Chapters 26-30* and LW54: *Table Talk Recorded by Anthony Lauterbach and Jerome Weller No. 3523.* See also 1 Esdras 4:42 – though previous verses of this text talk about how men cannot live without women and that women rule over men.

assumption, we need only to look up "feminine" in Webster's Dictionary. Despite his misogynist and patriarchal language,[11] I do not believe we should assume that Luther is against homoeroticism. It is very telling that he was aware that it is existed, but never spoke strongly against it (except as it pertains to femininity). The root of Luther's bias against male effeminacy is his disdain for all femininity.[12]

Luther's condemnation of effeminate men also applies to those who are heterosexual. Luther believed that to choose or be forced to act like or take on the roles of women was equivalent to being cast off from God(dess) [Paul may be expressing similar prejudices in the book of Romans].[13] Addressing the strange gender word play that occurs in Genesis describing Jacob, Luther remarks: "But these, too, are declined in the feminine gender, even though they are of the masculine gender. Thus God allows Jacob to be cast off and to be subject to servitude that is disgraceful and unworthy of a free man."[14] Despite Jacob's sexuality and gender, the mere act of speaking/writing about Jacob in a feminine way signals disgrace to Luther.

In contemporary society, our culture and media continues to believe that the worst insults that can be hurled at a man are

---

[11] While rooted in the Genesis story, the easiest way to see Luther's disdain for femininity is summed up in his belief that women can become like men, but men do not become like women: "The result is that the husband differs from the wife in no other respect than in sex; otherwise the woman is altogether a man. Whatever the man has in the home and is, this the woman has and is; she differs only in sex and in something that Paul mentions 1 Tim. 2:13, namely, that she is a woman by origin, because the woman came from the man and not the man from the woman." Luther continues to argue that men have a more perfect nature then women. [LW1: *Lectures on Genesis: Chapters 1-5*]

[12] Luther lectures that women are "foolish for the most part" [LW 54: *Table Talk Collected by Conrad Cordatus No2938b.; see also Table Talk Recorded by Veit Dietrich No. 439]* and compares nuns to sterilized swine, while monks are like horses who keep their testicales [LW5 : *Table Talk Recorded by Conrad Cordatus No 2981b.]* Spayed sows were called *Nonnen*, or nuns. Gelded horses were called *Mönche*, or monks. Actually, of course, the animals were named after monks and nuns and not the other way around (highlighting that Luther's patriarchy is rooted in the conventions of his time).

[13] Luther attributes these same misogynistic assumptions to Paul in LW25: *Lectures on Romans.*

[14] LW5: *Lectures on Genesis: Chapters 26-30: Genesis 29:29*

derogatory terms for femininity and female sexual organs. And as much as we may wish we were not a part of it, it is also the culture of our church. Faithful Lutherans and congregations all over the country still have a hard time talking about things other than what female clergy are wearing or how they are styling their hair. And we wonder why we still have a hard time providing female clergy with equal pay and opportunity, or uttering the feminine descriptions of God(dess) that are throughout scripture.

Where contemporary bibles list "homosexuality" (which in most cases means gay male sex) as a vice, Luther lists effeminacy as the root of unclean and unnatural vices. Contemporary readers need to remember that Luther was familiar with same sex relationships, and that he could have chosen to explicitly talk about them as innately unnatural. Instead Luther argues that the feminization of men is the real issue. In quoting scripture Luther lists "homosexuals" as immoral (1 Cor. 6:9) but, note that his focus and concern is effeminacy:

> *To uncleanness to the dishonoring of their own bodies among themselves.* From the apostle this vice gets the name **uncleanness and effeminacy**. Thus we read in 1 Cor. 6:9: "Do not be deceived; neither the immoral, ... nor adulterers, nor the effeminate, nor homosexuals, etc., will inherit the kingdom of God"; and in Eph. 5:3: "All uncleanness, or covetousness, must not even be named among you, as is fitting among saints"; and in 2 Cor. 12:21: "They have not repented of the uncleanness, immorality, and licentiousness which they have practiced." He also calls this a dishonor, or shame; for as the nobility of the body (at least in this respect) consists in chastity and continence, or at least in **the proper use of the body, so its shame is in its unnatural misuse.**[15]

What are these unnatural misuses of the body that Luther is concerned with? Luther continues to very clearly state that uncleanness and effeminacy are interchangeable:

---

[15] LW25: *Lectures on Romans.*

The **uncleanness, or effeminacy**, is every intentional and individual pollution that can be brought about in various ways: through excessive passion from shameful thoughts, through rubbing with hands, through fondling of another's body, **especially a woman's**, through indecent movements, etc. I have called it "intentional" in order to differentiate it from the pollution that takes place during the night and sometimes during the day and the waking hours, but which happens to many people involuntarily. Such things are not intended. I have called it "individual," **for when it becomes heterosexual or homosexual intercourse, it has a different name**.[16]

Did you notice that Luther is very clear that he is not talking about "homosexual intercourse"? In fact, he notes that he is especially talking about heterosexual "fondling of bodies."

Why would it be considered effeminate for a man to touch a woman's body in a way that causes orgasm (hence the comparisons to wet dreams) and to spilled seed?[17] For Luther, sex outside of marriage was fornication and sin. Effeminacy was sex inside or outside of marriage in which the male was not the top (the penetrating dominate partner) and in which procreation was not the aim of the act. Anything other than procreative sex inside of marriage was just one of the sins of Sodom, which for Luther included: "adultery, fornication, effeminacy, and even incest."[18] Before contemporary readers use Luther's view of fornication and effeminacy as a means to discount everything but unprotected coital sex within marriage, we should remember that Luther's understanding of marriage was not as "conventional" and "traditional" as we would like to believe. For example, Luther and Melanchthon advised the head of the Smalcald League Phillip of Hesse to enter a bigamous marriage.[19] Luther believed that bigamy

---

[16] Ibid.

[17] See Sowing your Seeds in Goodsoil

[18] LW3: *Lectures on Genesis: Chapters 15-20*.

[19] In Phillip's case, Luther came to regret the advice he gave after he learned about the existence of a concubine and of venereal disease. However Luther also gave similar advice in the matter of King Henry VIII's divorce. [Gritsch, Eric W., Martin- God's Court Jester: Luther in Retrospect, Fortress Press, 1983, 79.]

was more favorable than divorce, because "bigamy was acceptable to God as a 'Turkish marriage.'"[20] Luther not only believed that marriage was defined by civil authorities, like many contemporary queer people who get married in other states or countries, he actively sought out most liberal marriage laws.

It would be easy to say that Luther did not understand passion because he was not initially attracted to his wife, though he later learned to love her. Thankfully, Luther's call to celibacy changed, causing his opinions about sexuality to change and give birth to the Reformation and our Lutheran confessions.[21] Today, our Lutheran leaders know that it is important and often times necessary for those who are not called to celibacy to have a partner. It is time for us to continue the Reformation that Luther started and renounce the misogyny and patriarchy that taints our confessions.

The Lutheran church no longer believes that women are inferior to men, so why do we continue to pass along the idea that effeminacy is inferior by prohibiting gay and lesbian Lutherans from serving on both sides of the communion table? We must untangle the roots of our tradition from the thorny soil of sexism.

Misogyny and Patriarchy in the Bible

Misogyny and patriarchy is not only a problem for Luther and the writers of our confessions, it has also been written and translated into our scriptural texts. Recognizing this problem, Ken Stone, encourages readers to critique the parts of the bible that are rooted in patriarchy, violence, homophobia and heterosexism and turn to safer texts. Stone does this by focusing on more holistic texts found in and outside the biblical canon using these countertexts to challenge other more patriarchal violent texts.

The first safer text that Stone examines is the Song of Solomon. Using the rubric of Carole Vance, Stone seeks to focus on the pleasure and gratification women have in sexual intimacy and to move away from a focus on the patriarchal structure of this biblical text. Stone states that, "So long as conditions of gender

---

[20] Ibid.

[21] See Why Luther Decided to Have Sex

inequality and oppression exist (as they certainly did in ancient Israel, and as they continue to do today), the situation of women with respect to sexuality will always be one in which the <u>tension</u> between pleasure and danger must constantly be kept in mind."[22] By analyzing the text from today's standard that cares about women's sexual gratification the meanings that can be drawn from this text counter and challenge the history of patriarchy.

However, because the biblical witness has many distinct voices, it is possible not only to critique the biblical texts for our context today, but Stone is also able to root his critiques in countertexts. Showing the pleasure of sex for women, Song of Songs is a countertext that challenges more oppressive texts in the bible. To the many texts that show sex as a danger to women or women as a danger because of their ability to seduce others to have sex the Song of Songs offers a more enlightened position of women and their sexuality.

Song of Songs offers a women's perspective on sex and is possibly even authored by a woman. In the Song of Songs, sex is intimately linked with the consumption and enjoyment of food. Though food and sex can be linked together in many places in scripture, the Song of Songs uniquely uses metaphors of eating and food to show the orality and delight of sex outside of the explicit bounds of marriage. This sensuous text offers a powerful eroticism that challenges the tradition that often demonizes sexuality and women at the same time.

Another text that links sex and food is Ecclesiastes (Qohelet). Though Qohelet is more embedded in patriarchal thinking than the Song of Songs, unlike the Song of Songs, Qohelet explicitly links the enjoyment of sex and food with the favor and will of God(dess). Qohelet believes that being good and wise does not always produce happiness in a world ruled by fate. Because Qohelet believes that being too good and too wise may not be fruitful, Qohelet argues that it is the enjoyment of food and sex that is approved by God(dess).

---

[22] Stone, Ken, <u>Practicing Safer Texts</u>, Pre-Published version given to students in the Fall 2005 online class Queer Exegesis in the Hebrew Bible,183.

Stone's analysis of Song of Songs and Qohelet, makes it possible for him to argue that justice demands that all be able to enjoy food and sex. And because both Song of Songs and Qohelet do not explicitly require that the enjoyment of sex happen in marriage and it is especially clear that sex is not directly linked to procreation, it is easy to see how these biblical countertexts can support queer claims that justice also requires that queer individuals (who, to continue the food theme, could be said to have different sexual tastes) also enjoy sex.

Stone's method of critiquing the biblical witness, while also lifting up alternative biblical voices as safer texts, is a valuable method for a queer reading of the bible. I believe this method is also an invaluable way to read the bible, particularly for the gender queer.

The majority of queer theorists rarely do more than play lip service to the gender queer by including transgender in their list and then go on to only talk about the dynamics of sexual preference rather than self sex/gender preference. Those who do take up the subject, generally, only talk about societal constructs of masculinity and femininity or butch/femme constructs and never begin to touch subjects of the greatest concern to the gender queer including: gender performitivity; genetic sex variations; gender plurality; anatomical sex; anatomical sex reassignment; and post modern sexuality.

Those who self-identify as transsexual (pre-operative and post-operative), passing, transgender, gender queer and/or gender plural can find safer texts and textual readings extra biblically that speak powerfully to their experience. Deeper study of some of the female men of God(dess) provides volumes of safer texts. Many female monks, who had an understanding of sexual dimorphism without the ability/desire to change their anatomical sex found the Gospel of Thomas to be an illuminating text. Margot King tells of a monk, Amma Sara, who says to her fellow monks, "I am a woman in sex but not in spirit."[23] Rooted in Galatians 3:28's claim that "there is neither male nor female: for you are all one in Christ

---

[23] *The Sayings of the Fathers* X, 73

Jesus,"[24] the donning of a monks robe and the taking of a masculine name was thought to be a commandment from God.

The church fathers,[25] in the 4th century, believed that women were only able to become pleasing to God if they would give up their sex and become men for the sake of their soul. According to Vern Bullough statements such as those above may be an indication that the "Christian Church, to a certain extent, encouraged women to adopt the guise of men and live like men in order to attain the higher level of spirituality normally reserved for men." He goes on to say that, "Transvestism among women was usually admired and only rarely punished."[26] The female men of God(dess) were able to find countertexual support to critique alternative biblical voices (Deut. 22:5).

Another extra-biblical safer text is the Acts of Theckla (September 23). A close examination of the text reveals that Theckla tries to increase her power even further by cross-dressing to look like a man. Theckla is burned at the stake, after her mother testifies against her. In the tradition of Hananiah (Shadrach), Mishael (Meshach), and Azariah (Abednego) in Daniel 3, who survive the fiery furnace Theckla is unharmed by the fire. Theckla then goes to Paul and proclaims: "I will cut my hair off and I shall follow you wherever you go. (chapter 25)" This could be seen as an act of mourning similar to the actions of women in the Old Testament, especially because Theckla tears Alexander's cloak [which is also a sign of mourning (chapter 26)]. However, Theckla also "pulled off his crown and made him a laughing-stock" (chapter 26).[27] Using the conventions of the honor/shame dynamic, a theme that runs throughout the text, Theckla intentionally disgraces Alexander and ceases power.

Theckla's true intentions are reveled in chapter 40, when Theckla cross-dresses in a man's cloak and goes to Paul. As Theckla puts on the cloak of a man, zie[28] also takes on the power of

---

[24] KJV

[25] St. Ambrose (August 11) and St. Jerome in particular.

[26] Bullough, Vern L. *Transvestites in the Middle Ages*

[27] This would have increased Theckla's power and decreased the power of Alexander.

[28] Zie/Zir is a gender queer set of pronouns that attempts to imply gender that is both

a man. (Paul creates an environment that allows women to take control of their own bodies and sex lives.) Theckla extends the liberation of power even farther when she fully takes on the power given to men, by cross-dressing.[29]

While the countertexts that I examine are not specifically linked to food and eating, I believe that viewing sex/gender in the same light as food will prove useful for the gender queer. As Stone lifted up, Song of Songs uses apples as a euphemism for sex. Apples are also a wonderful euphemism for anatomical sex and gender. Though some people may only recognize two types of apples (red or green) there is really a wide variety of apples (Fuji, Granny Smith, etc.). In the same way, some people may only recognize two sexes (male and female) there are actually more than 48 scientifically recognized genetic sexes (XX, XY, XXY, etc.), many varieties of anatomical sexes (male, female, intersex, eunuch, etc), and many variations of hormonal sex.[30] Our bodies, gender and understandings of our sex is as evolutionary and diverse as apples.

Gender also evolves like apples. Botanists believe that apples evolved from roses. The transformation of the rose into an apple is like the gender transformation of some gender queer individuals through sexual reassignment (desired or undesired). Intersex individuals, who are assigned a sex at birth may relate to the story of the division of the intersexed Adam into a male Adam and female Eve (a story that is also linked with the apple).

---

male and female. I am using Zie/Zir when the life of the individual seems to exist as both male and female. In cases where an individual identifies as either male or female I will try to use the pronouns that they self identity, however this is difficult since the stories are typically written with heteronormitive assumptions.

[29] This brings to mind Paul's declaration that in Christ there is no longer male or female and the Gospel of Thomas' assertion that women can become men after baptism as Theckla only takes on the appearance of a man after she is baptized, which could be because of Greek understanding that Spirit + water = sperm that was upheld by many of the female monks [see legend of Euphrosyne and legend of Eugenia in Anson, John. Viator v.5. *The Female Transvestite in Early Monasticism*].

[30] These variations of hormonal sex are illuminated by the large number of people who take estrogen (birth control) or testosterone (Viagra) in order to maintain "normal" bodily functions. Hormonal balances also change in a person's lifetime (menopause is one example where women take hormonal therapy).

Stone's analysis of the Song of Songs and Qohelet, as a countertext that affirms the pleasure of sex and food, has useful implications for gender queer individuals and communities. By bringing together the biblical affirmation that compares sexual pleasure to the pleasure of eating, and specifically the eating of apples, with the biblical affirmation of gender and gender transformation offers a powerful model for queerness not just in terms of sexual preferences but in terms of gender construction. This is a bold move for queer exegesis as it is powerfully inclusive and addresses issues of both sexuality and gender construction that are important within and outside of the queer community. I will continue to use countertexts to pull out the queer themes, characters and symbols of our sacred scriptures throughout the rest of this text.

Solid Rock Foundations:
The Queer Sex Life of Martin Luther

"A solitary man is either a beast or a god." (Homo solus aut deus aut daemon)
– Martin Luther[31]

---

[31] <u>LW2</u>: *Genesis 13:3*

Luther's Sex Life as a Model for the Church

What is more foundational to our faith than the life and writings of Martin Luther? Like all of us, Luther was both a saint and a sinner, as noted in the previous chapter. While our contemporary church has spent millions of dollars and decades studying sexuality, we do not seem have spent any time studying the sex life of Luther himself. Luther's journey from sexual rigidity to an openness to marriage and fatherhood is a wonderful model for our own Lutheran church that seems uncertain about how to move from its own sexual rigidity to a place of embracing the diversity of Lutheran families that exist in our church.

While I cannot show that Martin Luther believed that queerness was normal, his stance on queer sexuality and gender is not very different from some of the other beliefs that Luther held strongly that contemporary Lutherans have departed from and in most cases repented from (like urging the death of the Jews, Mennonites and peasants).

Thankfully, contemporary Lutherans have found ways to disagree with some of Luther's bigoted beliefs, in order to follow the call of the living Gospel. Despite these beliefs, most contemporary Lutherans have seen the value of ordaining women who are called by God(dess) to ordained ministry. At first glance, it would seem that Lutherans could use the same process of discernment about the ordination of queer individuals who are called by God to ordained ministry as they did to decide to call women.

Unfortunately, sex seems to get in the way. (The Lutheran churches that currently allow queer individuals to become ordained require them to be celibate.) Some Lutheran Bishops will allow non-celibate queer pastors to work on the professional roster until they become "partnered" or "committed." This presumes that sex only happens in a life-long committed relationship, but what the Bishops really mean is: "tell me when you are having sex."

How did it become all about sex? Scripture tells us that people who are highly sexual are often the most called to deliver God(dess)'s message. King David had more than 700 wives and

300 concubines and we all know what happened with Bathsheba, and yet this was God(dess)'s chosen. I'm certainly not saying that the church should look the other way when it comes to the sexual ethics of its clergy members; we have certainly seen what has happened to the Catholic Church when they chose to do this.

I wish Lutherans cared as much about how faithfully queer people share the Good News or how diligently they serve the sacraments, as Lutherans care about what queer people do (or do not do) with their genitals. A friend of mine, who is a Franciscan nun, once asked me why the Lutheran church cares so much about what queer people do with their genitals. She said: "I don't understand; the sacraments are served with the hands, not the genitals in the Lutheran church, right?"

It is not only the contemporary Lutheran church that cares about genitals, Luther did too. Luther believed that the natural order was for a man to be drawn to women.[32] However, according to his own standard of what was natural, Luther was queer. Luther was not naturally drawn to women (not even the woman who became his wife). Luther was quite contented to a life of celibacy. Instead, Luther chooses not to do what is natural to him and ends up getting married for political reasons and in order to prove the point that given the choice between celibacy and serving the Gospel that we all ought to choose to have sex.

Why Luther Decided to Have Sex

> Everything in Luther's background indicates that the decision to enter a monastery was not hastily made even if the incident which forced a decision was impromptu. Much against his father's will. Luther entered the monastery of the Hermits of St. Augustine, which was by far the strictest of the religious houses of the city. There is a solid core of evidence in his lectures, sermons, letters and Table Talk that Luther took his vows seriously and even went beyond the ordinary requirements of the Rule. Both during his career as a monk and later in life he attacked those monks who sought 'exemption' from the strictest observance of the Rule.[33]

---

[32] LW3: *Lectures on Genesis: Chapters 15-20.*

How does a man who entered one of the strictest monasteries and followed his vows even more strictly,[34] decide to abandon his vow to celibacy, get married and have sex? It appears that Luther's decision to get married was made just as abruptly as his decision to take the vow[35] in the first place. However, Luther's journey from a person called to remain celibate to a person called to marry, have sex and become a father is a long one. It took Luther more than two years to follow his own advice and break his vow of celibacy. Luther decided to have sex,[36] in part as a rejection of the authority of the pope and papal priests and in order to embody his own rhetoric against monastic vows. But, the crucial factor for

[33] Senn, Franck C., "Lutheran Spirituality," Protestant Spiritual Traditions. Ed. By Senn, Franck C., Paulist Press, New York, 1986, 13.

[34] Luther wrote: "I had been called by terrors from heaven and become a monk against my own will and desire (to say nothing of the inclinations of the flesh!): I had been beleaguered by the terror and agony of sudden death, and I made my vows perforce and of necessity." [Luther, Martin, "Letter to His Father: Dedication of On Monastic Vows (21 November 1521), A Reformation Reader: Primary Texts with Introductions, Ed. Janz, Denis R., Fortress Press, Minneapolis, 1999, 77.] See also: Luther, Martin, "Luther on His Monastic Life," A Reformation Reader, 77; Senn, 13.

[35] Luther decided to enter the monastery one night when lightning frightened him and he vows to St. Anne that he would enter the monastery if he survived. Luther wrote: "I had been called by terrors from heaven and become a monk against my own will and desire (to say nothing of the inclinations of the flesh!): I had been beleaguered by the terror and agony of sudden death, and I made my vows perforce and of necessity." [Luther, "Letter to His Father," 77.]

[36] It should be pointed out that it is impossible to say when Luther first had sex. There is not much known about Luther's sex life. That he had sex is certain, because the product of his sexual intimacy was seen in the life of his children. Because Luther often argued that sex was a fundamental part of marriage, in this paper Luther's decision to get married and his decision to have sex will be examined together. As Luther stated: "'Marriage consists of these things: the natural desire of sex, the bringing to life of offspring, and life together with mutual fidelity.'" [LW54:Table Talk Recorded by Veit Dietrich (between February and March, 1932), 25.] Though we know that Luther thought sex was an essential part of marriage, we still cannot accurately discern when Luther first had sex. Though traditionally, the first sexual experience happens on the eve of the wedding service, the Luther's may have been interrupted from their coitus:

"Even on his wedding night, Luther couldn't refuse a person in need. At 11 p.m., after all the guests had left, radical reformer Andreas Karlstadt knocked at the door. Largely because Luther fiercely opposed him, Karlstadt had fled town. But now, when Karlstadt was fleeing the Peasants' War and needed shelter, Luther took him in." {Galli, Mark, "Little-Known or Remarkable Facts about Martin Luther's Later Years," Christian History, Vol. 12 Issue 3, p2-4, 1993 [EBSCO Online Religion & Philosophy Index].}

Luther was a personal call to marriage from Katy and his belief that his call from God(dess) had changed.

Anticlericalism

Why is anticlericalism important to a discussion on celibacy and sex? The character of rhetoric is that it affects people beyond the page. Luther was a charismatic leader who had the ability to tell people even when and when not to kill.[37] Luther's words and writing had power and historical evidence suggests that politics and anticlericalism played a role in Luther's writings and in his decision to reject the vows of celibacy.[38]

Anticlericalism is "a repudiation of the clergy as any sort of intermediary between God(dess) and humanity, including its role as a mediator of the divine Word."[39] The idea of the priesthood of all believers led to strong anticlericalism, which may have started with clerics who questioned papal authority and was violently enforced by the populace.[40] While Luther's charismatic preaching and rhetoric helped create an anticlerical movement that Luther was strongly opposed to, Luther participated in anticlericalism[41] when it

---

[37] Luther had influenced people to kill on many occasions, including his influence over the fate of the Mennonites. But, the most notorious is his influence in the pheasant war (1524-1526), which is often considered the greatest uprising in Europe before the French Revolution. Pheasant's who were influenced by Luther's rhetoric, did not use nonviolent methods of persuasion that Luther encouraged, so "[Luther] urged the princes to "smite, strangle, and stab [the peasants], secretly or openly, for nothing can be more poisonous, hurtful, or devilish than a rebel. It is just as when one must kill a mad dog; if you do not strike him, he will strike you and a whole land with you."" { Edwards Jr., Mark U., "After the Revolution," Christian History, Vol 12. Issue 3, 1993, 8-13 [EBSCO Online Philosophy and Religion Index].}

[38] Goertz, Hans-Jurgen, "'What a Tangled and Tenuous Mess the Clergy is!' Clerical Anticlericalism in the Reformation Period," Anticlericalism in Late Medieval and Early Modern Europe, Ed. Dykema, Peter and Oberman, Heiko A., Studies in Medieval and Reformation Thought, Volume LI, Ed. Oberman, Heiko A.J, E.J. Brill, New York, 1993, 509. See also: Dipple, Geoffery L. "Luther, Emser and the Development of Reformation Anticlericalism," Reformation Anticlericalism, 1996, 50.

[39] Dipple, Geoffrey, Antifraternalism and Anticlericalism in the German Reformation: Johann Eberlin von Gunzburg and the Campaign against the Friars, Scholar Press, 1996, 11.

[40] Goertz, 501.

[41] Luther's first anticlerical act was participating in a book burning in Wittenberg after his

suited his needs:[42] "Luther tried to distance himself from anticlerical diatribes and he toned down his language against clerics, although by 1523 Luther had come to appreciate the value of anticlericalism as a polemic tool, and that he was willing to exploit it when this seemed necessary."[43]

Asserting that Luther's anticlericalism was a polemic, should not infer that anticlericalism was a peripheral part of Luther's theology. Geoffery Dipple argues that "[Luther's] anticlericalism was, therefore, not peripheral to his Reformation theology. The rejection of the papal priesthood was an integral part of the attack on the sacramental system of the medieval church."[44] Luther's anticlericalism extended beyond his belief in the priesthood of all believers:

> The starting point for Luther's attack on the clergy may have been his soteriology and the doctrine of the priesthood of all believers. But for many of his contemporaries this was the endpoint; only gradually did they come to realize the full anticlerical implication of his teachings. And they were brought to his realization as

---

books were banned by the Catholic Church [Goertz, 509].

[42] Luther's feelings toward the pope and the papal priests shift depending upon the type of rhetoric he was using. In his 1520 letter *To the Christian Nobility of the German Nation Concerning the Reform of the Christian Estate*, Luther articulated the link between the priesthood of all believers and anticlericalism: "It is pure invention that pope, bishop, priests and monks are called to spiritual estate while princes, lords, artisans, and farmers are called the temporal estate." [Luther, Martin, "To the Christian Nobility of the German Nation Concerning the Reform of the Christian Estate" A Reformation Reader, Fortress Press, 1999, 91.] Also in 1520, Luther wrote in *The Freedom of a Christian*: "I freely vow that I have, to my knowledge, spoken only good and honorable words concerning [the pope] whenever I have thought of [the pope]." [Luther, Martin, "The Freedom of a Christian," A Reformation Reader, 98.] Luther did not praise the pope because he believes that the pope and the priests are correct, but because he believes that the pope will hear his words understand his true role in the church. Luther writes: "You [the pope] are a servant of servants, and more than all other men you are in a most miserable and dangerous position. Be not deceived by those who pretend that you are lord of the world..." In 1537, Luther wrote in the *Smalcald Articles* that "the pope is the real Antichrist who has raised himself over and set himself against Christ for the pope by his own power, which amounts to nothing sine it is neither established nor commanded by [God(dess)]." [Luther, Martin, "The Smalcald Articles," A Reformation Reader, 1999, 127.]

[43] Dipple, Antifraternalism and Anticlericalism, 16.

[44] Dipple sites Luther's *On the Missuse of the Mass* to prove his argument [Ibid, 55].

much by more traditional anticlerical forms as by the inner logic of Luther's theology.[45]

Luther's anticlerical rhetoric was very sophisticated, and was extended in many directions that Luther never intended. In Luther's writings he was only attacking papal priests; he is not against all priests. Luther's objective in his anticlerical writings was to reform the priesthood. Luther wanted to motivate the church, pope, priests and nuns to reorient their relationship with God(dess) and follow the example of Christ, because he firmly believed that the churches hierarchy placed an unnecessary mediator between humans and God(dess). Luther writes: "For this rock stands unassailed: 'I am the way,' and there is none other. Any other way is wrong, slippery, and dark."[46] Because celibacy was one of the vows of the papal priesthood, part of Luther's rejection of celibacy was a call to priests to reject the vows deemed necessary by the pope. Luther writes in the *Smalcald Articles*:

> The papists had neither authority nor right to prohibit marriage and burden the divine estate of priests with perpetual celibacy. On the contrary, they acted like antichristian, tyrannical, and wicked scoundrels and they gave occasion for all sorts of horrible, abominable, and countless sins, in which they are still involved...We are therefore unwilling to consent to their abominable celibacy, nor shall we suffer it.[47]

Luther's rejection of the vow to celibacy was in part a rejection of the authority of the pope and papal priests as much as it was a rejection to the vow itself.

Vows & Celibacy

While anticlericalism encouraged Luther to condemn monastic vows, Luther was affected by the lives of the clergy. "As lay people grew more active in the life of the church, they held the

---

[45] Ibid, 13.

[46] LW44, 254.

[47] Luther, "Smalcald Articles," 137.

clergy to a higher standard. For many, it was no longer acceptable if parish priests, despite the church's rule on celibacy, had women who were wives in everything but name."[48] Luther believed that clergy should be released from vows that they were incapable of holding because vows were unnecessary (though sometimes useful). Luther argued that the only completely valid vow is a vow to the gospel, the same vow that one takes in baptism.

Despite Luther's rejection of monastic vows, he believed that chastity could play a role in the life of the faithful, but celibacy is only a small minority. "Luther thus clearly differentiated between a true and false chastity. True chastity concentrates on faith in the [God(dess)] who loves sinners. False chastity relies on human merit and self-righteousness rather than on [God(dess)'s] unconditional love for the [unGod(dess)ly] in Christ."[49] In Luther's *On Monastic Vows (1521)*, the discernment of what is a true vow was essential. One can make a vow in order to be faithful, but they should never make a vow in order to become privileged or holier. "[A person] is not at liberty to take vows or set [him or herself] under oath or a compulsory rule of life. And, if a [person] has taken the vows already, [he or she] must neither fulfill them nor keep them, but must be released and set free."[50]

On Monastic Vows also argues that chastity was an individual calling that could only be considered as a matter of free choice independent of an individual's call to ministry:

> If you obey the gospel, you ought to regard celibacy as a matter of free choice: if you do not hold it as a matter of free choice, you are not obeying the gospel. It is quite impossible to make an evangelical counsel into a precept, and it is equally impossible for your vow to be a counsel. A vow of chastity, therefore, is diametrically opposed to the gospel.[51]

---

[48] Tracy, James D., Europe's Reformations, 1450-1650, Rowman & Littlefield, New York, 1999, 19.

[49] Gritsch, 161.

[50] Luther, Martin, "The Judgment of Marin Luther on Monastic Vows: LW 44: 245-264, 326-337, 392-396," [www.wls.wls.net/students/coursematerial/Reformationhistory/LutherReadingProject/Chapter…], Electronically Retrieved (4/3/2004).

[51] Luther, Monastic Vows.

Beyond Words to Between the Sheets

Luther's rejection of vows and celibacy went beyond rhetoric Luther actively encouraged "numerous regular clergy to renounce obedience to their superiors, to break their vows and to shape their lives anew."[52] Yet, Luther continued his strict discipline that he had undertaken at the monastery and he viewed his own life as one of celibacy[53] and proclaimed: "They will not push a wife on me!"[54]

Commenting on his choice to remain celibate, Luther remarked: "'It is not that I do not feel my flesh or sex, since I am neither wood nor stone, but my mind is far removed from marriage, since I daily expect death and punishment due to a heretic. Therefore I shall not limit [God(dess)'s] work in me, nor shall I rely on my own heart."[55] Luther viewed his single status as a calling from God(dess) to be celibate.

So why did he eventually decide to get married and have sex? "Because, Luther asserted, he had become convinced that getting married was one more testimony to the rediscovered gospel – the 'good news' that [God(dess)] in Christ will triumph over sin, death, and the evil so strongly manifested in the papal church's self-righteousness."[56] However, Luther's decision does not seem to be motivated purely by anticlerical motives. Luther truly changed his mind about all the reasons he felt called by God(dess)[57] to remain celibate:

---

[52] Goertz, 508.

[53] Senn, 13.

[54] Luther, Martin, "Letter to George Spalatin, Watrburg, August 6, 1521," LW 48,. Luther also responded in a similar manner to Philip Melanchthaon, who appears to be trying to persuade Luther to marry, exclaiming: "But I shall be quite careful with you, that you don't succeed!" [LW48: "Letter to Philip Melanchthon, September 9, 1521."]

[55] Gritsch, 158.

[56] Ibid, 159.

[57] "Nevertheless, [God(dess)], who has taken me out of the monastery, has placed me now not in a pretended [sic] monastic service but in the true service of [God(dess)]." [LW48: "Letter to Hans Luther, November 21, 1521."] See also: Edwards Jr., Mark U., "After the Revolution," Christian History, Vol 12. Issue 3, 1993, p. 8-13 [EBSCO Online

I also did not want to reject this unique [opportunity to obey] my father's wish for progeny,[58] which [God(dess)] so often expressed. At the same time, I also wanted to confirm what I have taught by practicing it; for I find so many timid people in spite of such great light from the gospel. [God(dess)] has willed and brought about this step. For I feel neither passionate love nor burning for my spouse, but I cherish her.[59]

It was God(dess)'s call, rather than Luther's attraction to Katherine of Bora (Katy),[60] that caused him to change his mind, get married and have sex.[61] Though it was not Luther's attraction to Katy that originally struck him, Luther later in his marriage finds himself deeply in love with his wife:[62]

> When Martin Luther married, neither he nor his bride," Katherine von Bora, felt "in love." Katherine was still getting over a broken engagement to a man she truly loved. And Martin admitted, "I am not 'in love' or burning with desire." Yet their love for each other blossomed throughout their 20-year marriage .[63]

> Just as [God(dess)] called Luther to marry, Katy also called Luther into marriage: "He had met Katie, as he called her, and eight other apostate nuns during the Easter season of 1523. He tried to help them to survive and to find

---

Philosophy and Religion Index].

[58] "You were determined therefore to tie me down with an honorable and wealthy marriage." [LW48: "Letter to Hans Luther."]

[59] Gritsch, 159.

[60] Luther was against marring because of lust: "Some marriages were motivated by mere lust, but mere lust is felt even by fleas and lice. Love begins when we wish to serve others." [Luther, Martin, "A Monk Marries" Christian History, Vol. 12 Issue 3, 1993, 24 [EBSCO Online Religion and Philosophy Index].

[61] In his table talk discussion, Luther stated: "'When one looks back upon it, marriage isn't so bad as when one looks forward to it." [LW48: "Table Talk Recorded by John Schlaginhaufen (between June 12 and July 12, 1532)".]

[62] "'I'm rich.' Said Luther. 'My [God(dess)] has given me a nun and has added three children.'" [Ibid.]

[63] Galli, p2-4.

husbands for them. He succeeded in arranging marriages for the eight nuns, but Katie resisted all his attempts to match her with someone else."[64]

Katy played an instrumental role in Luther's decision to get married. In fact, Katy's insistence that she not marry anyone other than Luther (or his friend Nikolaus Amsdorf) seems to be the most influential factor in Luther's decision to get married. Luther's parents had been against his clerical vows from the beginning, but this alone had not persuaded Luther to marry. Luther had remained celibate for more than two years after he published his position against monastic vows. It was only when Katy refused to marry anyone else that it was finally the right time for Luther to marry.

Conclusion

Luther's journey from a person called to remain celibate to a person called to marry, have sex and become a father is a long one. While some may argue that if Luther can go against his natural inclination (celibacy) and marry a woman, that queer people should do the same and marry a person of the "opposite sex." But, this would be an improper analogy, as Luther's struggle was not an issue of orientation, it was about celibacy. More bluntly, Luther decided to have sex. Luther's story does not give us a model to discern our sexual orientation and it does not teach us how to pick our life partner, it teaches us to discern if we should have sex.

Most people (at least non-queer people) do not have to think about the political implications of their marriage or decision to have sex. Most people get the luxury of a private life, queer Lutherans in professional ministry are expected to report to candidacy committees and bishops and let them know whether or not they are having sex and if that call changes. To put this in perspective, pastors do not have to report if their Christological understandings change, or how faithful they are in their prayer life, but queer pastors have to report whether or not they are having sex.

---

[64] Gritsch, 60-61.

Luther's process of deciding to have sex, speaks loudly to our contemporary church. Celibacy is a rare gift, one that is not connected to the call to ministry. Luther states very clearly, that we are given the choice between following the Gospel, or the churches policy of celibacy. I urge all queer Lutherans (who are able) to do what Martin Luther did: choose to have sex for the sake of the Gospel.

Our Lutheran Core:
Christ and our Queer Salvation

[The devil says,] 'Behold, you are weak. How do you know, therefore, that God is gracious to you?' Then the Christian must come and say, 'I have been baptized, and by the sacrament I have been incorporated [in Christ]; moreover, I have the Word.'

"The devil objects: 'This is nothing, for many are called, but few are chosen' [Matt. 22:14]…

But a Christian says, 'I wish to do as much as I can, but Christ is the bishop of souls. To him will I cling, even if I sin.' It is thus that one has assurance.[65]

– Martin Luther

---

[65]LW54, 86-87.

Queerly Saved

"What a queer bird!"[66] *— Martin Luther's interpretation of what the disciples think of Jesus when Christ says that the disciples must eat the bread that Jesus is.*

"It impressed them as a queer and odd sermon; they thought it unheard-of that He should give His flesh as eternal food and His blood as eternal drink".[67] *— Martin Luther*

While Martin Luther is the foundation of Lutheranism, st the core of Lutheran faith is Christ. And at the center of Christ is our salvation, which we continue to experience bodily through communion. This moment, according to Luther was originally labeled queer. While Luther was not specifically talking about Christ's sexuality or gender in his comments, he was talking about an expression of a countercultural lifestyle that can easily be compared to the countercultural lifestyles that have caused some people to name gay, lesbian, bisexual, transgender and others queer.

In this chapter, I will begin to explore the saving acts of Christ by looking at my Lutheran heritage. Then, I will examine how these roots are shaped by liberation, lesbian feminist liberation and queer theology. The result is an understanding of the saving act of Christ that not only addresses the concerns of our postmodern world, but that also provides Good News for to Lutheran queer people and their allies.

Lutheran Heritage

Ancestrally, I am a Scandinavian, German and English Lutheran who can confirm my Lutheran heritage all the way back to a baptism in Germany that took place in 1648.[68] Culturally, I am a

---

[66] LW23: *John 6:55.*

[67] LW23: *John 6:66 (see also 6:61).*

[68] Sievert Janssen Schulte[68] was baptized on December 20, 1685 at the Völlen Evangelische-Lutheran Church in Völlen, Leer County, Ostefriesland, Hanover.

Midwesterner who spent the first 21 years of life in South Dakota. For me, "Lutheran" has been more of an identity then a list of things I believe. Consequently, it is easier for me to explain my faith by talking about stories of Darlene Audus, my grandmother then to use the typical theological language you may expect to find. The following is patchwork quilt that begins to form a theology of salvation (justification by grace, through faith in Christ), through the life and works of Martin Luther, Dietrich Bonhoeffer and Darlene Audus.

Martin Luther

Martin Luther views justification as liberation from our sins in the now and not yet (causing us to be simultaneously a saint and a sinner). The liberating death and resurrection of Christ grants us freedom to "be a sinner and sin boldly, but believe and rejoice in Christ even more boldly.... No sin will separate us from the Lamb, even though we commit fornication and murder a thousand times a day."[69] At the same time that we can be assured that we are justified, we are also called to be faithful.

Luther believes faith is three things: 1) "hearing the word of promise"[70] in the Word of God(dess) (especially preached);[71] 2) unity with, or marriage to, Christ;[72] and 3) "the only key by which the hidden mystery of the cross may be unlocked."[73] First, a person hears the Word and has faith. Then, the believer understands the Word because of their faith. Because of the centrality of the Word, the cross is crucial to faith:

> The [God(dess)]who is crucified is the [God(dess)] who is hidden in [God(dess)'s] revelation. Any attempt to seek [God(dess)] elsewhere than in the cross of Christ is to be rejected out of hand as idle speculation: the theologian is forced, perhaps against [their] will, to come

---

[69] LW2, 371; LW48: *Letters I*, 282

[70] McGrath, Alister E., Luther's Theology of the Cross: Martin Luther's Theological Breakthrough, Blackwell, 1985 174.

[71] "Concerning Christian Liberty,"117-118; and McGrath, 174.

[72] "Concerning Christian Liberty," 125; and McGrath, 174.

[73] McGrath, 175.

to terms with the riddle of the crucified and hidden [God(dess)].[74]

❦ Just as the cross is a crucial part of faith, so too is suffering. Both God(dess) and humans suffer for the same purpose: to bring believers to God(dess). Because suffering is key to the experience of faith, God(dess) is active in suffering both on the cross and in the suffering of believers.[75] Luther calls suffering a "precious treasure," because he sees God(dess) hidden in suffering "working out the salvation of those whom [God(dess)] loves."[76] Believers suffer "Anfechtung: [God(dess)] assaults [a person] in order to break [them] down and thus to justify [them]."[77] Alister McGrath describes the state of Anfechtungen in the following way:

> Luther's understanding of the condition which [a person] must meet if [they are] to be justified can be defined in terms of self-abasement and crying out to [God(dess)] for grace. Once [a human] fulfils this condition, [God(dess)], in [God(dess)'s] righteousness, may be relied upon to be faithful to [God(dess)'s] promise of grace...[78]

Through grace, suffering and the Word of God(dess), the believer finds faith and "by the pledge of [their] faith in Christ, the believer becomes free from all sin, fearless of death, safe from hell, and endowed with the eternal righteousness, life, and salvation of [their] Husband Christ."[79] This is true justification and liberation, by grace, through faith that ends all suffering.

---

[74] Ibid, 161.

[75] Ibid, 151.

[76] Ibid, 151.

[77] Ibid, 151. There are multiple sources of Anfectungen for Luther, but because this essay is about justification and soteriology it is primarily concerned with Luther's understanding of the cross and the ways that Anfectungen applies to justification and soteriology. Luther's connection of Anfectungen with the devil is connected to the temptation to sin that is continually in an individual's life (LW 51:179-180). However, since justification allows us to "sin boldly," I am choosing not to address the type of Anfectungen that tempts people to sin.

[78] Ibid, 107.

Dietrich Bonhoeffer

Dietrich Bonhoeffer views humans in a fallen world where sin and shame break community with God(dess). The Holy Spirit, who brings Christ to the individual, overcomes this brokenness. Christ takes our punishment, which undoes[80] our sin, and brings the individual into a position to have union with God(dess).[81] The relationship between the individual and other humans also follows this same process, for unity with the other is not possible without God(dess). Unity with the other comes from the unity of the Spirit, for it is only in Christ that we can completely love the other. All of this is possible through faith in combination with God(dess)'s will.

Bonhoeffer takes Luther's idea of justification by faith one step further. Like Luther, the cross is central to Bonhoeffer's understanding of justification, however Bonhoeffer adds a communal component to justification:

> All are in [God(dess)] and yet each remains distinct from [God(dess)]. All are united with each other, and yet distinct. Each possesses [God(dess)] totally and by themselves in the grace-filled dual solitude of seeing truth and serving love, and yet never is solitary because they always live only within the church-community. But we shall see not-only [God(dess)] but also [God(dess)'s] church-community. We shall no longer merely believe in its love and faith, but see it.[82]

Because we are free for and free from others[83] we are free to have union with whomever we choose. The rub is that we will be judged by God(dess) based on our connections. Bonhoeffer writes: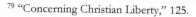

---

[79] "Concerning Christian Liberty," 125.

[80] Because Christ's actions occurred in the past, sin is has already been justified. This is explained more in depth in <u>Christ the Center.</u>

[81] This is similar to Luther's concept of marriage with God(dess), but it has more to do with returning to the state of nakedness with God(dess) that existed before the fall and can be found again when we are united with Christ and shame is conquered.

[82] <u>Sanctorum Communio</u>, 289.

[83] This idea of freedom is also articulated by Luther in "Concerning Christian Liberty," 115.

[God(dess)'s] judgment and grace apply to persons. This means that judgment and grace apply to all individual persons within the church-community-to the plurality of spirit as described above-to marriages and friendship that have become part of the sanctorum communio, and finally to the unity of these, the collective person of the church-community, the unity of spirit.[84]

This multi-level judgment allows humans to be both condemned and accepted by God(dess): "[God(dess)] can condemn a collective person and at the same time accept individuals who are part of it, and vice versa, is an idea that is as necessary as it is incomprehensible."[85]

The communal component of Bonhoeffer's vision of justification means that humans can and should take upon themselves the sins of the other. This is the role of the church community, for it is in the church community that "we see the love that voluntarily seeks to submit itself to [God(dess)'s] wrath on behalf of the other members of the community, which wishes [God(dess)'s] wrath for itself in order that they may have community with [God(dess)], which takes their place, as Christ took our place."[86] This means that a member of the church-community should not judge other members in the community, but instead seek to allow the other to put God(dess) at the center, just as Christ brings God(dess) to our center.

Through the grace of God(dess), in our faith we are saved by God(dess) both individually and in relationship to the communities we are bound to. So, our faith gives us freedom (free for and free from), calls us into right relation, and union, not only with God(dess), but also with our neighbor as a part of the sanctorum communio (community of saints).

Darlene Audus

[84] Sanctorum Communio, 287.

[85] Ibid, 286. Bonhoeffer cautions that this should neither confirm nor deny the idea of universality, because God(dess)'s judgment is incomprehensible.

[86] Ibid, 184.

When I think of justification by faith, I think of my grandmother, Darlene Audus. Darlene is a child of the depression who believes that every person has the ability to do good things in the world. When Darlene goes to rummage sales she buys things she will never use. In fact, she rarely buys anything for herself at all. With 6 children, 12 grandchildren, and 7 great grandchildren, Darlene has plenty of people to buy for. Darlene has two rooms in her house that are mainly used for storage of all the things that people might be able to use someday. Sometimes, Darlene will let us look around and see if there is anything that we need. Other times, she will put things in special places that will be given to us someday as a gift.

Darlene is the happiest person I know, even though she has lived most of her life doing things for other people. She is also deeply saddened when other people are suffering. She does everything in her power to help people get the things that they need. One time, when I was in a car accident and I was in the hospital, Darlene drove over 200 miles to sit next to my bedside. She told me it was worth it, because even though I slept the whole day, I knew she was there. It was not enough for Darlene to hear that I was okay; she wanted to see it for herself.

But the thing I will always remember about Darlene is how she feeds people. Darlene cooks food all day and then feeds more than a dozen of her children, grandchildren and great grandchildren. The entire meal, Darlene will serve people and (if she can get away with it) she will never sit down and eat. The older folks try to get Darlene to sit down and enjoy the meal that she has cooked, but she always refuses or sits down for a couple of seconds and then hops up to get something for someone. The older folks do not know why she does not sit down, but I know the secret. Darlene does not sit down at the dining room table and eat because she is too busy eating the food that the kids at the kid's table do not want to eat. The parents say to their kids: "you better eat all of those peas, or you won't get any dessert." And, "did you finish all your food yet?" Then, when the parents are not looking Darlene will eat their peas, and bring the kids dessert. For those children, eating peas is the most unimaginable suffering they can think of. Darlene cannot see any reason not to relieve the suffering of others, especially when it involves doing something she loves in a way that nourishes her body.

How My Understanding of Salvation/Justification is Shaped by my Lutheran Heritage

My understanding of justification by faith is a combination of the ideas presented by Luther, Bonhoeffer and Darlene. From Luther, I have learned that the Word and the cross are crucial to faith. It is through the Word that I first discovered that God(dess) loves and justifies me.

However, because I learned from Darlene that suffering is something that should be avoided; I had a hard time accepting that suffering for the sake of God(dess) or by God(dess), is ideal or necessary. It did not make sense to me that God(dess) would want to send God(dess)'s Son to suffer for me or that God(dess) would want me to suffer so that I could have faith. Luther's description of Anfechtungen seems too much like an abusive father that "assaults" people and "breaks them down" for their own good. While this description of God(dess) reminds me of my earthly father, I do not think it is ethical to describe God(dess) in this manner. What message does it send to a woman in an abusive relationship if this is our example of how faith is developed in a loving relationship? How can I, as the victim of an abusive alcoholic father, love a God(dess) who treats me the same way? What can I say about the Christians who threw holy water on me, sang hymns when I was around and tried to beat the gay demons out of me, so that I could be saved? My experience and deepest convictions will not let me believe that God(dess) assaults me for my own good.

While I do not think God(dess) wants me to suffer in order to have faith, I do believe that God(dess) used suffering for my justification.[87] God(dess) loved humanity so much that God(dess) became human and suffered with and for humankind and me so that humankind and I are and will be resurrected with God(dess) into eternal life. Because I have been justified, I can "sin boldly." This does not mean that I want to sin, or that I choose to sin.[88]

---

[87] However, if God(dess) had asked my opinion, I would have encouraged God(dess) to seek other means.

Rather, it means that my sin is forgiven, or undone, even before I confess them, because of the crucifixion and resurrection of Jesus. However, I am an active sinner, because I am given the power to "sin boldly" with the promise that I am and will be justified.

However, I cannot stop with my own justification. I am compelled both by Bonhoeffer and by Darlene to also long deeply for the justification of others. Because I can rest assured in my salvation, I am free to speak truth to power and strive to diminish, deflect and eliminate the suffering of others. This should be done with caution and care not to diminish the agency of other people with attention to the particular ways that God(dess) is calling us to do justice, love kindness and walk humbly by eating peas so others may enjoy dessert.

I am justified, liberated and made free (free for and free from) not because of my suffering, but through the suffering of Jesus Christ on the cross. My faith is the belief that God(dess)'s grace is the agent of this justification. And, my response to justification is to "sin boldly" and discern the ways God(dess) is calling me to be a part of the saving work that God(dess is doing until my justification extends beyond myself to all of creation.

Queering Lutheran Understandings of Salvation

Just as I am shaped and formed by my Lutheran heritage, I am also shaped and formed by my status as a transgender lesbian feminist. In this section, I will look at the understanding of salvation as presented in liberation, lesbian feminist liberation and queer theology.

Liberation Theology

Liberation theology purports that God(dess) is on the side of the suffering, as depicted in the Exodus story and the suffering of Christ on the cross. It is difficult to list common beliefs of liberation theology, because the understanding of who is suffering

[88] The extraordinary Rev. Steve Sabin of Christ Church Lutheran where I was an intern would add here that God(dess) forgives us all our sins, even the sins we do that we knew were sinful and even if we enjoyed it.

changes based on what population is writing the theology (South American, American Indian, Asian, Black, Womanist, Gay, Lesbian, Queer, etc.). I have drawn on John Allen and Peter Phan for my conception of Liberation Theology.

After studying nine distinguished liberation theologies, John Allen found four common ideas that are critical to the movement: 1)the "preferential option for the poor:"[89] the church removes its alliance from affluent social structures and realigns with the poor who demand justice; 2) "institutional violence:"[90] acknowledging that the current social arrangements evoke violence on millions through oppression and forced poverty; 3) "structural sin:"[91] "Structural sin" is the belief that communal sin is important and that the church has an obligation to act against communal sins; and 4) "orthopraxis:"[92] counteracts orthodoxy or right belief with the idea that right action is more important.[93] Allen also points out that liberation theologians understand that they must work with social structures in order to achieve justice and that they act in pastoral dimensions (because they have an obligation to share and counsel to others).

Unlike Allen, Peter Phan does not believe that liberation theologies should be lumped together and assessed. Phan notes that while diversities are important liberation theologians "are fellow travelers on a common journey, albeit through different routes to the same destination."[94] Phan believes that Liberation theology has an influential methodology that seeks the root cause of oppression and to end it through interreligious dialogue, storytelling, and a continual hermeneutical circle. Then, in hermeneutics liberation theologians can transform the "unjust word" and take an "advocacy stance.[95]" Stated simply, liberation

---

[89]John L. Allen Jr., "Key principles of liberation theology." National Catholic Reporter, June 2, 2000. InfoTrac Expanded Academic ASAP.

[90] Ibid.

[91] Ibid.

[92] Ibid.

[93] Ibid.

[94] Peter C Phan, , "Method in Liberation Theology," Theological Studies, electronically retrieved, InfoTrac: Expanded Academic ASAP.

[95] Ibid. With the use of the terms of Elisabeth Schussler Fiorenza.

theologians seek to end the false universalism of the church of the majority.

While Phan and Allen disagree about how the different liberation theology movements work together, they both argue that the church has a responsibility to not only interact with orthodoxy, but also to pay attention to its orthopraxis in the world as an extension of God(dess)'s saving activity in the world.

Lesbian Feminist Liberation Theology

Lesbian feminist liberation theology, according to Mary Solberg, is a call to allow experience, (strong) objectivity, and accountability for/from all people to change the myth of the collective experience.[96]

Much like other liberation theologies, lesbian feminist liberation theology understands the importance of praxis. Carter Heyward argues that because we are all a part of One Body an important component to being human is praxis.[97] Expanding on this, Heyward writes, "Our question is not when or how God will act to save women, men, and the earth itself, but rather when and how we will act."[98] Heyward values praxis because the body of Christ, the church and Christians are the embodiment of Christ alive and acting in the world. However, it is important to remember that praxis also comes with responsibility. Solberg extends the realm of the world's orthopraxis to both action(s) and non-action(s).[99] In this way the orthopraxis of the world is both shaped by what we have done and by what we have left undone.

Lesbian Feminist Liberation theologians propose that this can be done by reshaping the social science systems in the world including: economics, sex, gender, sexuality, cultural, class, race,

---

[96] Mary M. Solberg, Compelling Knowledge: A Feminist Proposal for an Epistemology of the Cross, State University of New York Press, 1997, 37-53.

[97] Carter Heyward, "Living for the Living" Speaking of Christ: A Lesbian Feminist Voice, ed. Ellen C. Davis, Pilgrim Press, 1989, 29.

[98] Ibid, 42.

[99] Solberg, 1-9, 50-53, 125-159.

---

ethnic, and abused. For this reason, Christ (both the historical and living body of Christ) is with the suffering.

Lutheranizing Liberation and Lesbian Feminist Liberation Theology

Lesbian feminist liberation theology is one lens for looking at the social systems in the world. But, I believe that liberation theology fails to represent the saving work of God(dess) for two reasons: 1) liberation theology does not account for the salvation of oppressors or the oppressed once they are liberated; and 2) the dualistic separation of the oppressed and oppressor is not an earthly reality, because we are all simultaneously oppressed and oppressors (saint and sinner).

Luther's work calls me to again look at the saving work of the historical Christ. Luther argued that we are all equally oppressed and all oppressors in our sin, because we are all equally condemned by the commandment, "thou should not covet."[100] In the equality of our sin, we are seen by God(dess) unmarked by the dividing lines of economics, sex, gender, sexuality, culture, class, race and ethnicity. This means that no one is actually queer. And, while we have the ability to work as God(dess)'s continuing salvation in the world, only the historical life, death and resurrection of Christ can act as the complete saving act of God(dess).[101]

Queer Theology

Like liberation theologians, queer theologians identify with the saving work of God(dess) in the Exodus story and in the suffering of Christ on the Cross. However, queer theology envisions God(dess)'s historical saving actions through Christ as queer in two ways: 1) Christ's praxis was/is queer; and 2) Christ's sexuality was/is queer.

---

[100] Martin Luther, Basic Luther: Four of His Fundamental Works, Templegate Publishers, Springfield, Il, 119.

[101] This is because temporally it is Jesus life, death and resurrection that sets in motion my justification, which in turn enables me to strive for my neighbors health, wholeness and justification. While it is true that my participation in God(dess)'s saving actions in the world is one of the ways that Christ is alive and resurrected in the world through the body of Christ (the church/community of saints), with out the salvation and justification that I get from Jesus I am unable to get beyond my own needs to helping my neighbor.

Christ's praxis is queer because it confronts the majority's heterosexist,[102] patriarchal and oppressive political structures. Robert Goss highlights the queer praxis of Christ, in his book <u>Jesus Acted Up</u>:

> It was not God's will that Jesus died to ransom those with sin. This was a Christian interpretation of the death of Jesus. Rather, the cross symbolized the violent and brutal end of Jesus in the context of his political praxis for God's reign. Jesus was executed by the political infrastructure of Jewish Palestine as a political insurgent. The Jewish religious aristocracy and their Roman rulers perceived Jesus' message and practice of God's reign as a threat to the political order... His death embodied his own vision and commitment to practice God's reign to the very end.[103]

According to Goss, Christ's queer praxis saves queer people from spiritual violence by illustrating: 1) that HIV/AIDS is not God(dess)'s punishment for gay people; and 2) that gay people are called to sexual intimacy as saved and fully embodied people.

Like Goss, Leslie Addison also recognizes the liberating power of the queer praxis of Christ:

> [Jesus] was a transgressive, he was disruptive. He was killed in attempt to silence voices crying for change. Christ was resurrected, continues to be resurrected, by a [God(dess)] who is more powerful. He is a reminder to us that we can expect opposition, but that we can also count on the grace and dunamis[104] that we need to overcome it.[105]

---

[102] See Luke 7, Chapter 1 where Jesus cures a centurion's slave. The text says that it is a slave that is the most favored one, which probably meant it was the centurion's gay male lover. Jesus cures the man without ever seeing the centurion, without ever seeing the gay male lover and proclaims at the end that not even in Israel has Jesus found such faith.

[103] Goss, 75-76.

[104] Dunamis is Greek term, meaning "power."

[105] Addison, Leslie Katherine, <u>Passionate In-Queeries: Towards a Lesbian/Bisexual/Gay/Transgender Christology</u>, (PSR Thesis) 1996, 74.

Both Addison and Goss view the saving praxis of Christ as a call for queer individuals and communities to strive for orthopraxis, to use the historical Christ's saving praxis to perpetuate the unending saving orthopraxis of the resurrected body of Christ.

In addition to Christ's queer praxis, queer theologians also imagine Christ's sexuality is/was queer. According to Hayward, viewing Christ as a queer person is part of a universal longing to create a familiar God(dess). She further concludes that "it is not wrong to create theological and Christological images of ourselves. In fact, it is vital to our well-being and to our taking responsibility for what we are doing in the name(s) of God(dess)."[106] Envisioning a queer Christ, is a tool that helps queer Christians see that God(dess) is with them in their suffering and that Christ identifies with the sexually oppressed. For, as Goss writes:

> If the Christ is not queer, then the incarnation has no meaning for our sexuality. It is the particularity of Jesus the Christ, his particular identification with the sexually oppressed, that enables us to understand Christ as black, queer, female, Asian, African, a South American peasant, Jewish, a transsexual, and so forth. It is the scandal of particularity that is the message of Easter, the particular context of struggle where [God(dess)'s] solidarity is practiced. [God(dess)] and the struggle for sexual justice are practical correlation in a queer Christology.[107]

Goss imagines that Christ is queer, not only for queer people, but also for heterosexuals. If a straight person can imagine that Christ is queer, their likelihood of maintaining and promoting heterosexism will decrease.

One tool for envisioning Christ as queer exists in the gospel of Matthew. Christ's claim: "as you have done it to the least of these, you have done it to me" presents the easiest way to imagine Christ as queer. In our society, heterosexism purports that queer people are "the least of these." In light of the Matthew text, it could be said that denying queer people rights, denying their place

---

[106] Hayward, 19.

[107] Goss, 85.

in the priesthood of all believers, beating them, spiritually abusing them, creating special rules and rituals for them, and failing to seek justice for queer people is not only done to queer people, but it is also done to Christ.

A Queer Lutheran Understanding of Salvation

God(dess) loved humanity so much that God(dess) became human and suffered with and for humankind so that humankind is and will be resurrected with God(dess) into eternal life. Because I have been justified, by grace through faith, I can "sin boldly." This does not mean that I want to sin, or that I choose to sin. Rather, it means that my sins are forgiven, or undone, even before I confess them, because of the crucifixion and resurrection of Christ. However, I am an active sinner, because I am given the power to "sin boldly" with the promise that I am and will be justified. Consequently, I am free to discern the ways God(dess) is calling me to participate in the saving work that God(dess) is doing, until my justification extends beyond myself to all of creation. The queer Christ's physical suffering on the cross liberates us/me from our/my suffering as we act as both the oppressed and oppressors. And, though we are simultaneously saints and sinners, Christ's queer praxis calls us all to orthopraxis that seeks to end the suffering of all beings in the cosmos.

Queer Christology

... (homo) denotes Christ exclusively and on both sides no one could take away from me, although many would like to. – Martin Luther[108]

A queer Christology must go beyond queering understandings of salvation and speaking metaphorically about Christ as queer. Temporally there are three realms that show Christ's queerness: Christ's life and resurrection; the clothing of Christ that covers the baptized body of Christ (each of us); and the promised bodily presence of Christ in heaven. As I look at the queerness of Christ, I will focus scripture, the practices of the earliest Christians and Lutheran confessional understanding.

I have limited my focus in this way, because I could not possibly talk about the queerness of each and every person who is a part of the body of Christ. Even if I could, it would require me, you and everyone else in the world to be honest about how we differ from societal expectations about our gender and sexuality.

The Queer Historical Christ

In fact, many ancient and contemporary readers and scholars have noticed the queer sexuality and gender of the historical Christ found in our sacred scriptures. In Theodore Jennings' The Man Jesus Loved: Homoerotic Narratives from the New Testament, Jennings makes a convincing argument that it is possible to re-read the gospels[109] in light of Jesus' male beloved. This is a bold work of theology that brings out an important

---

[108]"Homo" is Latin for "man." Luther is not intending to call Christ a homo, I include it here to be intentionally provocative. [LW11: First Lectures on the Psalms II: Psalms 76-126: (Psalm 87:6).]

[109] This reading could also be extended into the entirety of the New Testament. I would like to see an extended re-reading of the Pauline texts (beyond the marriage section) from this perspective.

scholarly analysis of the queer narratives contained in the gospels that Jennings argues have been systematically ignored by heterosexist scholars.

Jennings' reading is centered on the mystery of the "beloved disciple," and the proposition that the beloved disciple was Christ's male lover. First, Jennings establishes how Jesus' relationship with his beloved can be read as a homoerotic relationship without doing violence to the text. The Gospel of John has the most hints of a sexually queer Jesus. In John, Jesus has a male whom he loves (called the beloved). The intimacy between Jesus and the beloved is seen clearly during the Last Supper in chapter 13. Imagine the scene: Jesus is reclining with the man he loves at a meal with friends. During the meal, the intimate details of his journey to the cross are revealed to the beloved.

Though Jennings is unable to discern the beloved's identity, he is able to link the beloved to crucial moments in the passion story: the last supper, the crucifixion and the empty tomb. Jennings' biblical scholarship convincingly argues that the beloved disciple was Christ's gay lover, that Christ was queer acting and that the truth of this may have been masked within the gospel texts.

Jesus is not only sexually queer, Jennings' also says Jesus has "troubling gender," and shows that Jesus' acceptance of gender transgression is clear in the gospels. One aspect of Jesus' gender that presents as queer is his willingness to go to wells (a space for women to do their work) and to associate with male water carriers (i.e. men who take on the roles society has delegated to women). Jesus is tolerant of traditional "men's work" and "women's work" being done by either and both genders.

Jennings' reading of the gospel relies on the historical queerness of Jesus. This means that if new historical evidence emerges to disprove the historical queerness of Jesus, the framework of this theology is negated. I believe that in order to have a queer theological/exegetical framework, Jennings' re-reading of the gospel needs to be read with an additional understanding that Jesus is queer today, both in praxis and in sexuality,[110] even if Jesus was not historically queer.

---

[110] See Addison, , 74; Goss, 75-76; and Heyward, 19.

Baptized Bodies: Female Men of God(dess)[111] and the Male Brides of the Female Christ

The Queerness of Christ extends beyond Christ's own physical body, through baptism as the act of being clothed in Christ trans-formed the bodies of women and men celebrating the rite of baptism. While this section provides language for talking about the diversity of bodies and the transgender experience in our postmodern world, it should be noted these stories of liberation could also be read as stories of misogyny. While it is not possible to lift these stories out of the sexism and patriarchy that they were created in, I hope readers will reject the misogyny while remaining open to the words of welcome for trans individuals and communities.

After Jesus' death many stoics believed that because women more readily expressed feelings that they were not properly in control of their bodies. Men, the stoics believed, were more logical and in their head. During a time when fleshly things were considered sin and the mind, when controlled, was pious, it was determined that women could not be saved

The Gospel of Thomas records the disciples' questions about how it is possible for Mary to be saved. Jesus explains that Mary is able to find salvation because in baptism she takes on the male form (clothed or covered in Christ): "For every woman who makes herself male will enter the kingdom of heaven."[112]

The need for Mary's (and ultimately all women's) divine sex change is rooted not only misogyny, but also in linguistics. In Hebrew, the word for water was also used as a euphemism for "seed of man" or sperm. In Greek, combining the word for Spirit with the Greek for water, created the Greek word for sperm (or seed).[113]   This euphemism is made explicit throughout the

---

[111] Palladius (ca. 430) is the first author to refer to these saints as the "female men of God." For a more in depth study of these saints see: Hotchkiss, Valerie R., Clothes Make the Man: Female Cross Dressing in Medieval Europe, Garland Publishing, 1996. To learn more about how these saints were viewed by and interacted with the patristic authors of the time, read: Cloke, Gillian, This Female Man of God: Women and Spiritual Power in the Patristic Age, AD 350-450, Rouledge, 1995.

[112] The Gospel of Thomas

[113] "Semen, then, is a compound of spirit (pneuma) and water, and the former is hot air

46

Greek bible and in our Lutheran Confessions when Jesus is called the new seed/sperm or new Adam.

The church fathers,[114] in the 4th century, believed that women were only able to become pleasing to God if they would give up their sex and become men for the sake of their soul.

Remember the story of Theckla was highlighted in the first chapter? There are at least twenty "female" born saints who experienced either a divine sex change and/or became monks who lived, dressed and identified as "males"[115] or at least with male names [for more detailed stories about the lives of these saints and others, see the Extraordinary Prayer Calendar in the Appendix].

Several female born saints lived/dressed as men,[116] while Wilgefortis and Paula of Avila experienced miraculous sex changes in order to remain celibate and/or to avoid marrying a man. Christian woman in the Middle Ages were told based on the Gospel of Thomas and Matthew 22:30 that "if they embraced celibacy on earth, their reward would be to become males in heaven."[117] Other female born monks[118] lived as males for years and were made saints primarily because of their gender variance. Many of these saints refused to name the sex of their birth, even when they were put on

---

(aerh); hence semen is liquid in its nature because it is made of water." [Aristotle, On the Generation of Animals, 29, http://www.greektexts.com/library/Aristotle/On_The_Generation_Of_Animals/eng/973.html, Electronically Recovered]

[114] St. Ambrose (August 11) and St. Jerome in particular.

[115] Because contemporary understandings of gender did not exist at the time and the pronouns about these saints shifts and sometimes shows the transphobia of the authors recording it, it is hard to say with any certainty what the sex or gender of these saints was in their own understanding. I use the quotes to exacerbate the fact that a clear definition of male and female is hard to define in relation to these saints.

[116] Saints Anastasia/Anastasios (March 10), Theckla (September 23), Eusebia Hospitia, Joan of Arc (May 30)

[117] Omnigender, 116.

[118] Euphrosyne/Smaragdus (February 11), Apollinaria/Dorotheos (January 5), Mary/Marinos of Alexandria (February 12), Hildegonde of Neuss/Brother Joseph (April 20), Pelagia/Pelagio (June 9), Marina/os of Antioch (July 17), Marina/Marinos of Sicily (July 20), Theodora/Theodoros of Alexandria (Septermber 11), Athanasia/Athanasios of Antioch (October 9), Anna/Euphemianos of Constantinople (October 29), Matrona/Babylas of Perge (November 9), Saint Eugenia/Eugenios of Alexandria, Susannah/John, and Saint Euphrosyne.

trial, expelled or killed because of charges of rape or fathering a child.[119] And some (Mary/Marinos of Alexandria), even raised the children they were said to have fathered.

The link between baptism and gender variance was not limited to women. 12th century cloistered male saints, like Anselm, continued to associate baptism with trans-gressing gender roles when the male monks began to think of themselves as male brides of a mother/father Christ. These medieval Christians believed that the fulfillment of their baptismal call was to literally feed humanity with their breasts as a mother suckles a child.

Rooted in the Hebrew bible's naming of the male God(dess) who "speaks of himself as mother, bearing Israelites in his bosom, conceiving them in his womb (e.g. Isa. 49:1, 49:15, and 66:11-13)"[120] and the Wisdom of God(dess) as the divine feminine (Ecclesiastes 24:24-26), these saints expanded the Gospel of Matthew's imagery of Jesus as a mother hen (23:37) and wrote about the breast feeding Christ whose humanity was dependent upon the simultaneous nature of Christ's mother/fatherhood. Unlike the binary sex roles of our contemporary culture, "Medieval authors do not seem to have drawn as sharp a line as we do between sexual responses and affective responses or between male and female."[121] This fluidity of gender went beyond the belief that men could be feminine to the idea that men could take on physical characteristics of the female body while still remaining male.

[119] Apollinaria/Dorotheos (January 5), Mary/Marinos of Alexandria (February 12), Theodora/Theodoros of Alexandria (September 11), Saint Eugenia/Eugenios of Alexandria, and Susannah/John.

[120] Bynum, Caroline Walker, Jesus as Mother: Studies in the Spirituality of the High Middle Ages, University of California Press, 1982, 125.

[121] Ibid, 162.

Your Queer Body in Heaven

It could be said that the Christian tradition requires all people born female to become metaphorically gender queer, while some people born male chose to identify that way. But in the future, if Luther is right, we will all be gender queer:

> In the future life we'll have enjoyment of every kind and the whole earth will be adorned with many trees and all things that are pleasant to look at. If we have our Lord God we'll have enough. We'll be children of God. I don't believe that we shall all be of the same stature, and there will be no marriage; otherwise everybody will want to be a woman or a man.[122]

You may or may not identify as gender queer now, but you will be in heaven. Our Christ is queer, if not historically, then Luther says he will be/is in heaven. This queer body is part of what we proclaim at each Eucharist feast. It is what we put in our stomachs as a fore taste of the queerness feast that is to come. We are the many parts of this one queer body! Ready or not, queerness comes.

---

[122]_LW 54:_ *Table Talk.*

Sowing Your Seed into Goodsoil

Alongside Christ's queer flesh are his queer words. It could be argued that all of Jesus' radical messages against individualism, capitalism and his welcome for the stranger turn societal assumptions on their head (and thus are queer). In this section, I focus how the seed parables in the Gospel of Mark serve as a model for the Lutheran church to work towards acceptance of those who are queer.

First Parable of the Seeds in the Gospel of Mark[123]

Genesis 38:8-10

[8]Then Judah said to Onan, 'Go in to your brother's wife and perform the duty of a brother-in-law to her; raise up offspring for your brother.' [9]But since Onan - knew that the offspring would not be his, he spilled his seed on the ground whenever he went in to his brother's wife, so that he would not give offspring to his brother. [10]What he did was displeasing in the sight of the LORD, and he put him to death also.

Mark 4:3-20

[3]'Look! Listen! A sower went out to sow. [4]And as he sowed, some seed fell on the path, and the birds came and ate it up. [5]Other seed fell on rocky ground, where it did not have much soil, and it sprang up quickly, since it had no depth of soil. [6]And when the sun rose, it was scorched; and since it had no root, it withered away. [7]Other seed fell among thorns, and the thorns grew up and choked it, and it yielded no grain. [8]Other seed fell into good soil and brought forth grain, growing up and increasing and yielding thirty and sixty and a hundredfold.' [9]And he said, 'Let anyone with ears to hear listen!'

---

[123] My analysis of the parable of the sower draws heavily from: , Mary Ann, Sowing the Gospel, 1989, Fortress Press, 148-172.

10 When he was alone, those who were around him
along with the twelve asked him about the parables.
[11]And he said to them, 'To you has been given the
secret[*] of the kingdom of God, but for those outside,
everything comes in parables; [12]in order that
"they may indeed look, but not perceive,
    and may indeed listen, but not understand;
so that they may not turn again and be forgiven." '

13 And he said to them, 'Do you not understand this
parable? Then how will you understand all the parables?
[14]The sower sows the word. [15]These are the ones on the
path where the word is sown: when they hear, Satan
immediately comes and takes away the word that is sown
in them. [16]And these are the ones sown on rocky
ground: when they hear the word, they immediately
receive it with joy. [17]But they have no root, and endure
only for a while; then, when trouble or persecution arises
on account of the word, immediately they fall away.[*]
[18]And others are those sown among the thorns: these are
the ones who hear the word, [19]but the cares of the
world, and the lure of wealth, and the desire for other
things come in and choke the word, and it yields
nothing. [20]And these are the ones sown on the good soil:
they hear the word and accept it and bear fruit, thirty
and sixty and a hundredfold.'

Do the seeds in the parable of the sower have anything to
do with sex or semen? If we read the parable through the lens of
Genesis 38:8-10 it does. Further, I believe that the parable of the
sower not only has a sexual component that would have been
meaningful at the time that story was originally told, it also has
something to say to contemporary Lutherans as they discern
whether or not to ordain non-celibate queer individuals.

What did this parable mean when it was originally being
told? Who were the seeds on the path? Jesus tells the story of the
sower just after the Pharisees have come by as living representations
of seeds falling on the path. The Pharisees are the ones that would
have proclaimed the Genesis law that all seed (sperm) that falls on
the ground is an abomination. But Jesus' parable makes the life and
faith of the Pharisees fallen seed. Previously I have shown that that

in the Gospel of Mark, Jesus uplifts how people live with/for their neighbor above rules. Here again in this parable, the spiritually powerful, become the seed on the path are not good soil for Jesus' ministry.

Who then is the rocky soil? Jesus gives a pretty big clue when he names Peter, since Petros is the Greek word for "rock." The disciples prove that they are rocky soil when they flee during the time of Jesus' persecution and crucifixion. The disciples seem to get things, but they lack depth and longevity. The sexual part of their story is that the disciples fled their wives and their property when they decided to follow Jesus. This would have been paramount to giving up all of their sexual power. But, despite the fact that they have done this, they continue not to get it. I wonder if they reclaimed all of their sexual power after Jesus died and was resurrected (too bad the Gospel of Mark ends with out telling the post-resurrection story, so we'll never know).

Jesus is not as obvious about who he is talking about when he mentions the thorny ground. However, a couple chapters later in Mark comes the story of a rich young man, whom Jesus asks to sell everything he owns, give the money to the poor and follow Jesus. This rich young man hears the words of Jesus and receives it, but his desire for money and possessions strangle his ability to grow in faith and we never see the rich ruler in the story again.

And what does this have to say about sexuality? Jesus' call for the rich young man to give up his possessions would also have been a request to give up sexual power (like the disciples). At the time that the oral storytelling of Mark's gospel took place, masters who owned slaves were allowed to have sex with them. Similarly, those who owned a wife, could have sex with them (the wife would have been considered property). But to give up all property also meant to give up slaves, wives and money, which is equivalent to giving up all sexual power.

So who is the good soil? In Mark's gospel, the only people who stick with Jesus during the crucifixion and discover the empty tomb are the women who are far off on the hill watching the scene. Jesus eats with, heals and protects the sexual outcasts, sex workers, and those who have no power sexually or socially. And aside from the centurion at the end of the gospel and when Jesus calls Peter

"Satan," the only people that recognize that Jesus is the Messiah are the demons. According to Jesus' parable the ones who are good soil are the same individuals that the Pharisees would have condemned as abominations.

The parable of the sower is a radical story that illustrates the radical grace of Jesus. Those who are the most spiritually powerful are wasted seeds and those who are the most vulnerable and the most sexually questionable are good soil. All four of these characters are simultaneously saints and sinners. As Lutherans, we resonate with this state of being. We must remember that in our baptismal call God(dess) has named and claimed us. God(dess) pulls us into the fullness of our identity and encourages us to be members of the priesthood of all believers and calls us good no matter our social-economic status, no matter how much political or sexual power we have or whether we agree to be celibate. The Good News is this: All people are good soil for Jesus.

But in this story, like in our Lutheran heritage where we are simultaneously both saint and sinner, we too find ourselves cast as both wasted seed and good soil. Lutherans have baptized more than 5 million believers in the ELCA alone, proclaiming at each one of those baptisms that they are called into the priesthood of all believers. Yet we waste that seed, because we do not really believe it. Policies in Lutheran churches around the world discriminate against queer individuals who live the fullness of who God(dess) has called them to be. Luther planted over 292 seeds in his writings that celibacy and the call to ministry do not go together. More than 5 million times we have professed that the priesthood is for all believers. But what we profess with our lips does not match the actions of our church. How many more seeds will we continue to waste?

There is an organization called Good Soil (www.goodsoil.org) that works toward the full inclusion of people of all sexual orientations and gender identities in the Lutheran church. They argue that ALL people are a part of the priesthood of all believers and that there is no reason to exclude queer non-celibate candidates (that are otherwise qualified) from ordination and call. This was a radical message when Luther first fought for it, but it should not be such a radical message today. The members of

Good Soil express the simplicity of our core Lutheran belief and are certainly good soil.

But are we still wasting seeds? In the ELCA, more than 1.5 million dollars was spent studying homosexuality in order to keep things exactly the same.[124] The leaders of our Lutheran church are thorny soil, because even if they believe in their hearts that non-celibate queer Lutherans should be ordained, they have (for the most part) refused to give up their power, privilege and pensions and they continue to get ordained in Lutheran Churches that discriminate against queer people. They are the rich rulers who refuse to give up all that they have earned to let the seeds of truth and justice grow in our midst.

What about rocky soil? ELCA members are rocky soil, because with all of our good intentions, even though we study the issues and even though you are reading this book we merely have words. At the sight of persecution, at the fear of losing our power, our candidacy, our jobs, our place in the pews, being kicked out of our congregations (community or building), losing the financial support or getting censure we (for the most part) say nothing. Or if we do, we say it quietly to people who believe us. But that is not enough according to Mark's gospel. If we waste our seed we will not be the ones standing on the hill watching the crucifixion. We will not be the ones to witness the empty tomb.

As Lutherans, we are dropping our seeds all over the path and watching them get eaten by birds. We vote over and over again not to ordain and call all people who are faithful, who are qualified, who are called by their community. 292 wasted seeds. More than 5 million times we have baptized people into the priesthood of all believers and yet we still do not believe and in our fear of being faced with the fact that we are simultaneously saint and sinner we say nothing to no one because we are afraid.

The Second Parable of the Seeds

---

[124] This was for the current three year study, who knows how many millions more have been spent in all the studies that the Lutheran churches have about homosexuality since the 70's. I know the LCA had at least three studies of their own on the subject before the ELCA was even created.

Mark 4:26-9

He also said, "The kingdom of God is as if someone would scatter seed on the ground, □27□ and would sleep and rise night and day, and the seed would sprout and grow, he does not know how. □28□ The earth produces of itself, first the stalk, then the head, then the full grain in the head. □29□ But when the grain is ripe, at once he goes in with his sickle, because the harvest has come."

This second parable about seeds in Mark reminds us what every good Lutheran sings: to God(dess) be the glory. It is not by our own actions that reaping and sowing happens. We fool ourselves into believing that we can make and vote on rules to decide whom God(dess) has called, when really we can merely watch and wait to see what grows up from the seeds we have scattered. We do not know how or why God(dess) calls up pastors. We can train pastors and seminarians to be diligent, we can teach them the proper use and means of grace, we can discern their integrity and help them to more fully live in right relationship with God(dess), their neighbor and their family, but ultimately we know that God(dess) is the agent doing the growing. Isn't this why the ordination vows for pastors are "I do/will and I ask God(dess) to help me," rather than asking church members or voting members to do it?

To live together faithfully does not mean to learn how to not split the church, it means that it is our job to strive mightily to discern each day, each hour, each moment what God(dess) is calling us to do and to yearn with each step to take a step closer to God(dess). God(dess) gives and takes. It is a pastor's job to notice the ways that God(dess) is working in the world and to point to it; to point at the cross and help people to remember; to take people off the cross and remind them that the suffering has been done already, not so that they may do likewise, but to harken the day when all pain and suffering shall cease.

Our Lutheran church should not be plucking sprouts and calling them weeds. She should sleep and rise night and day caring for, nurturing and reaping the fruits of God(dess)'s harvest (pun intended).

The Third Parable about Small Seeds[125]

Mark 4:30-3

> [30] He also said, "With what can we compare the kingdom of God, or what parable will we use for it? [31] It is like a mustard seed, which, when sown upon the ground, is the smallest of all the seeds on earth; [32] yet when it is sown it grows up and becomes the greatest of all shrubs, and puts forth large branches, so that the birds of the air can make nests in its shade."

This parable reminds me of the story of the "sinful woman"[126] in the Gospel of Luke (7:36-50), where Jesus points out that those who have gained much, have more gratitude. This tort response to Simon must have shamed him. With his parable, Jesus points out that Simon, a Pharisee who is concerned with following rules and piety, is not living the Word of God(dess) as well as the "sinful woman." Remember, there was a time when the most unforgivable thing you could be was a woman. Yet somehow, even though we once believed that the most sinful thing you could be is a woman, they were allowed to be ordained.

The one thing most consistently articulated by Jesus in every Gospel as sinful, is divorce. And I can remember a time when divorce was one of the most sinful things you could do (particularly if you were a pastor). Luther even goes so far as to call divorced people "queer."[127] Yet somehow, even though Jesus says it is the most sinful thing you can be, we still allow divorced people to be ordained and to remain pastors.

---

[125] Most things in the Gospel of Mark happen in threes (like the disciples being alarmed because they don't have enough food to feed everyone even though the numbers they feed decrease each time), so it is not surprising that there are three parables about seeds.

[126] The name of the "sinful woman" is not mentioned, nor is she allowed to talk. She only listens to two men with power talk about her. This reminds me of the queer pastors and laity in the ELCA who are studied and voted on without the ability to have voice or vote in the conversation.

[127] LW21: *The Fifth Chapter of St. Matthew: Matthew 5:33*.

How can this be? Well, it is usually because our cultural assumptions about what is the most sinful thing changes as people and cultures change. The point of the mustard seed parable is that no matter how small your stature or the pedestal that society puts you on, your ability to produce fruit and bear the Gospel is extraordinary. While it may be the current whim to consider queer people to be the smallest or most "sinful" people, we can still be extraordinary pastors. And like the sinful woman in the Luke passage, for some female, queer and/or divorced pastors, it could be said that when much is given there is much gratitude. People who are lifted up to the level of equality tend to notice, to give thanks and to make the best of their opportunity. Like Simon, people who have always had the power and privilege of being a pastor, do not always seem to notice when their power and privilege affects others adversely.

However, it sends a powerful message when we size people up in our church(es). There are congregations that only get a white woman pastor if they cannot afford a married white male pastor. If they cannot afford a woman they may then consider a queer pastor, which they may or may not pay enough money to live in their neighborhood. And many congregations will never think of the worth of a pastor who does not come from European/Scandinavian roots, who is disabled or younger. Often times, these minority pastors end up having to become extraordinary pastors required at every moment to justify their place at the table, even when they are only allowed the crumbs from the floor (Mark 7:28).

This parable is for those whose eyes see others or perhaps even bits of themselves as small. The good news is that Jesus was wrong. The mustard seed is not the smallest seed in the world,[128] only in the world that Jesus knew. Those who label people "small" are wrong when they believe there is anyone outside of the priesthood or that there is anyone or anything that God(dess) cannot use for God(dess)'s purpose.

---

[128] There are orchid seeds that are as small as dust. Epiphytic orchids of the tropical rain forest produce the world's smallest seeds, up to 35 million per ounce.

Good News From Word Alone:
Queer God(dess) and the Queer Creation

[God(dess)'s] word alone avails here, as Paul says in II Corinthians 10[:4–5], "Our weapons are not carnal, but mighty in [God(dess)] to destroy every argument and proud obstacle that exalts itself against the knowledge of [God(dess)], and to take every thought captive in the service of Christ."[129]

-Martin Luther

---

[129] <u>LW45</u>: *The Christian in Society II* "Temporal Authority: To What Extent It Should Be Obeyed."

In the Beginning was the Word, and It Was Queer... Even Before the Fall

Before the Fall it was pure and was created and necessary for procreation. But now it is corrupted by original sin. It is not a harmless heat, as it was in the beginning; but it is corrupted by lust and concupiscence. -Martin Luther[130]

There seems to be a perception in the minds of many people (including Luther's) that there was a "good old days" a "history" or a "tradition" of the monogamous heterosexuality that is idealized in contemporary society and looks something like *Leave It To Beaver*. However, the truth is that the "good old days" never existed.[131] There are volumes of books written on how history, archeology, zoology and science show that queer people are normal, natural and have always existed. But as a Lutheran, the tradition of our sacred scriptures, confessions and Lutheran history are more compelling to me then the opinions of the secular world.

From the very first page, the Hebrew bible is a queer story that overflows with queer characters. In the first creation story of Genesis (1-2:3), a plural God(dess)[132] orders chaos by separating water from dry land, earth from the heavens, light from dark, etc. A Gnostic sect of the Naassenes, believe that this primordial fluid was a gender plural essence called bythos. It is from this gender plural chaos fluid that God(dess) separates male and female.[133]

---

[130] <u>LW 5</u>: *Lectures on Genesis: Chapters 26-30*; *Genesis 30:40*.

[131] Coontz, Stephanie, <u>The Way We Never Were: American Families and the Nostalgia Trap</u>, Basic Books, 2002.

[132] There is debate among scholars about whether the plural reference to God(dess) is a royal we that signifies the greatness of God(dess) or if there is more than one God(dess) being talked about. Though the royal we theory is plausible, historical criticism has indeed shown that the early Israelite religion was polytheistic and does not become monotheistic until the time of Moses or the Exile.

[133] <u>Cassell's Encyclopedia of Queer Myth, Symbol and Spirit: Gay, Lesbian, Bisexual, and Transgender Lore</u>, Ed. Conner, Randy, et al., 1997, 99.

However, most contemporary biblical scholars believe this creation story was written by the Priestly (P) author who was influenced by the story of Tiamat. In the Sumerian's creation story, it is the bloody separation of Tiamat's body parts that create the cosmos. She is literally the mother earth whose very womb makes up the world. Depicted as a dragon or a sea monster, Tiamat was ultimately raped and cut into pieces by the warrior Marduk. References in both the Hebrew and Greek Bible depict God(dess) as the one who controls the chaos of the sea and/or sea monster,[134] suggesting that the God(dess) of the Israel is the God(dess) who conquers Tiamat. Women loving women from the ancient Amazons to contemporary lesbian feminists have found meaning in the way Tiamat gave birth to the world by fertilizing her own body without the seed of a man.[135]

Many scholars believe that the Hebrew version of this ancient Sumerian story uses the Canaanite gods Athirat (Qudshu or Qadesh meaning the Holy One) and El (who becomes conflated with Yahweh or Jehovah). Athirat was the goddess of the waters who held a lily in one hand and a serpent in another. She is also depicted as having a younger consort named Ba'al, though she loved both women and men. It is easy to see how the queer Athirat, goddess of water, could be associated with the Hebrew image of a plural God(dess) separating the watery chaos and ordering the cosmos.

Just as the first creation story depicts a queer creating God(dess) and a queer body that is separated into an ordered cosmos, the second creation story (Genesis 2:4b-3:24) depicts another queer birthing of the cosmos with God(dess)'s queer birth of Adam. While it is true that "God created Adam and Eve, not

---

[134] Genesis 1:21; Exodus 14:16 – 15:21; Numbers 11:31; Deuteronomy 11:4; Joshua 5:1, 24:7; 2 Samuel 22:16; 1 Kings 7:23-44, 8:44-45; Nehemiah 9:9-11; Job 7:12, 26:12, 28:14, 38:8 &16, 41:31; Psalm 18:15, 33:7, 46:2, 66:6, 72:8, 74:13, 77:19, 78:13, 78:53, 89:9, 89:25, 93:4, 95:5, 106:9, 107:25, 107:29, 114:3, 136:13, 136:15, 148:7; Proverbs 8:29; Isaiah 9:1, 10:26, 11:15, 23:11; 27:1, 43:16, 50:2, 51:10 & 15, 63:11; Jeremiah 5:22, 31:35, 51:36; John 6:19; Ezekiel 26:5-19, Amos 5:8, 9:6; Jonah 1:4-15; Nahum 1:4; Habakkuk 3:8 &15; Haggai 2:6; Zechariah 10:11; Matthew 8:26-27, 14:26; Mark 4:39-41, 6:47-49; John 6:18-20; Acts 7:36 ; 1 Corinthians 10:1; Hebrews 11:29; Revelations 21:1

[135] Similarly Jesus, who is said to have been in the beginning in John's gospel, is also born of a woman without the seed of a human male. "Tiamat," Cassell's Encyclopedia, 323.

Adam and Steve," the story is clearly modeled after the story of Gilgamesh and his male lover Enkidu. The Epic of Gilgamesh, which scholars believe heavily influenced the writing of the Genesis creation stories presents themes from both Genesis creation stories. In The Epic of Gilgamesh (written around 2100 BCE) Gilgamesh needs intimacy, so the deity creates a male intimate companion named Enkidu. After Gilgamesh has a series of dreams interpreted by his mother that he will soon love another man "like a wife" the goddess Aruru creates a companion male for Gilgamesh out of clay. Gilgamesh's mother Ninsun not only approves of the relationship, but she adopts Enkidu as her own son. Rather than temptation from a snake, an apple and a question, Gilgamesh is tempted by a woman (Inanna/Ishtar) who tries to seduce him.   Inanna/Ishtar's attempts fail, though Enkidu dies soon after the encounter.

My religion professor at Augustana College in Sioux Falls, the Rev. Dr. Richard Swanson, once told me that he imagined that the violent story of Tiamat was created by the Jewish grandmothers who wanted a less bloody story to tell their grandkids. It is easy to imagine how those same Jewish grandmothers, who lived long before PFLAG,[136] may have had the same trouble telling a creation story that involves male homoerotism and loose women trying to seduce a happily married man.

Queerness is not a disruption of God(dess)'s creation, it is the intention. God(dess)'s creation is queer, as queer as the material God(dess) creates with. Later I will expound upon this idea and show how the earliest Jewish interpretations read "male and female" God(dess) created them queerly.[137] The remainder of this section will focus on how God(dess) did not stop using queer people for God(dess)'s work and creative purposes in the world after the fall, in fact many queer individuals have been considered saints and spiritual leaders because of, not despite, their queer sexuality and gender.

---

[136] Parents, Family and Friends of Lesbians and Gays

[137] Impatient readers may note the use of the word "and" rather than "or."

Divine Sex Changes in Genesis

When culture began to believe that men were superior to women, it reinterpreted the queer creation story into a story of a woman coming from a man in order to reinforce cultural assumptions. And for centuries, patriarchal assumptions continued to reinterpret and sometimes guide our scientific assumptions of sex and gender.[138]

Still, the earliest listeners and readers of our sacred scriptures believed that sex changes were a miracle of God(dess), beginning with the first sex reassignment surgery that was preformed by God(dess) trans-forming the intersexual Adam into a male Adam and female Eve.[139]

This first sex change was not the final act of creation that ended the need for any other sex changes. Ancient Israelites believed that there were more than two genders: male, female, barren women and Eunuchs.[140] While rejecting the assumption that you cannot be fully a woman or man if you cannot procreate, we must continue to lift up the sacred stories of the God(dess) who not only performs sex change miracles but uses gender queer individuals as agents of God(dess)'s work in the world.

The earliest readers of the Hebrew Bible believed that barren women and circumcised men were models of the androgynous ideal (like the Divine Androgen).[141] This means that God(dess)'s command that all men be circumcised could be said to be a requirement that all faithful believers undergo a physical sex change. Numerous barren women also received divine sex changes when God(dess) notices them and opens their wombs: Sarai, Rebecca, Leah, Rachael, Zulaikaha, and Hannah.[142]

---

[138] See Laquer, Thomas, Making Sex: Body and Gender From the Greeks to Freud, Harvard UniversityPress, 1992.

[139] The Jewish midrash argues that: "Men and women were originally undivided, i.e. Adam was at first created bisexual, a hermaphrodite." [Plaut, W. Gunther, The Torah: Genesis- A Modern Commentary, 1974, 24.] See also, Gottwald, N. K. 1985. The Hebrew Bible--a socio-literary introduction. Includes index. Fortress Press: Philadelphia

[140] Carden, Michael, "Genesis/Bereshit," The Queer Bible Commentary, Ed. Guest, Deryn, et. al., SCM Press, 2006, 27.

[141] Ibid, 33, 35 and 49.

[142] Ibid.

While the type of sex change that comes from circumcision or the opening of a womb seems very different then the surgical and hormonal sex changes that some transsexuals undergo, the story of Dinah's sex change may speak more to the contemporary transsexual experience.[143] This story begins with Jacob, a character so gender queer, that even Luther notices.[144] But, how could he not notice when the text seems to go out of its way to note that everything that Jacob does is feminine: female pronouns are used and it is noted that he "dwells in tents" (Gen 25:27) which were known to be the space of women. Even more queer is the fact that this effeminate male is able to amass so much masculine power, which the patriarchy of the time defined as the ability to "take" multiple wives and produce many male children.[145]

Jacob's children come as the result of at least two divine sex changes (Leah's womb is opened in 29:31 and Rachael's is opened in 30:22) and ultimately produces twelve male offspring, who become known as the twelve tribes of Israel. Though it's not recorded in the text, ancient readers believed that after eleven of the sons were born (six to Leah, two to Bilhah and two to Zilpah), that Leah prayed to God(dess) to have a girl so that her sister Rachael could bear Jacob's final male child, Joseph.[146]

While some sources believed that Dinah's sex change occurred in Leah's womb and others believed it was happened after Dinah was born they all agree that it was God(dess) who changed Dinah's sex from male to female. Yet most commentators fail to notice that the cost to Dinah for her divine sex change is the loss of the privileges given to men in a patriarchal society.[147] As a woman Dinah endures the subjugation commonly endured by other women of her time when she is raped by Sehecham (34:2-7) and "treated like a whore" (34:31). Dinah ultimately dies giving birth to Benjamin.[148]

---

[143] See Carden, 47-51.

[144] LW 5: *Lectures on Genesis: Chapters 26-30: Genesis 29:29*

[145] See Carden, 47-51 and Stone, Ken, "1 and 2 Samuel," The Queer Bible Commentary, 212.

[146] See Berakhot 60a and Tanhuma 19:5.

[147] Rosen, Tova, Circumcised Cinderella, 89.

Despite Dinah's unfortunate fate, the prayer of Leah has been used by trans individuals as model for praying to God(dess) for a sex change. Qalonymos ben Qalonymos in Even Bohan (1322) prayed:

> Our Father in Heaven! You who did miracles to our fathers by fire and water; you who turned [the furnace] in Ur of the Chaldees [cold] to stop it from burning [Abraham]; you who turned Dinah in her mother's womb [into a girl]; you who turned the rod [of Moses] into a serpent in front of tens of thousands; you who turned [Moses'] pure arm into a [leper's] white arm; you who turned the Red Sea into land, and the sea floor into solid and dried-up earth; you who turned the rock into a lake, the cliff into a fountain - if only you would turn me from male to female.[149]

The sex changes in Genesis could be read as enforcing strict gender binaries, as God(dess)'s way to trans-form the gender queer into "normal" procreative men and women. But, we have already seen how God(dess) uses Jacob in gender queer ways, without correcting or changing the ways Jacob is queer in gender. Michael Carden, who called Jacob a "pretty-boy nancy,"[150] describes Jacob's youngest son Joseph as "twitling, minicing, in rainbow garb and with painted eyes, Joseph is a flaming young queen."[151] God(dess) continues to use gender non-conforming individuals not only in the book of Genesis, but throughout our sacred texts.

YHVH's Same-Sex Marriage

Not only does the queer creating God(dess) intend a queer creation, but you also may be surprised to learn that in scripture

[148] Carden, 51.

[149] As it appears in Rosen, 87.

[150] Carden, 50.

[151] Ibid, 53.

same-sex marriages are considered sacred, while opposite-sex marriages are flawed and human. I imagine if the book of Hosea was framed in this way, that it would probably be studied and read more. But before getting too excited, I must note that Hosea is firmly rooted in phallocentric assumptions that presume male power and privilege that are enhanced by/through penetrative sex. While I affirm the queerness of the text, I continue to reject the misogynist and patriarchal assumptions that surround it.

It should also be noted that whenever I talk about the queer sexuality of God(dess), I am not assuming binary sexuality. Honoring the legitimacy of the bisexual experience and the ways sexual desire and orientation can change over a lifetime, when I talk about the queerness of God(dess) I am not presuming that God(dess) is either gay or straight. In typical Lutheran experience I believe that God(dess)'s sexuality can be both/and.

Growing up as a gender queer lesbian in South Dakota, I was often told that I was not a Christian, that I was going to hell, that I was an outsider and that if Jesus came again I would be one of the people identified as "Not my People" (Hosea 1:8). When friends and colleagues told me that the bible contained all of life's answers and that my life was clearly wrong, I often read them chapters 1-3 of Hosea. Then, I asked them if their understanding of the easy answers about God(dess) could explain why God(dess) would command Hosea to marry a female sex worker, to abandon her for being a sex worker and then take her back again.

I imagine that if any of my friends or colleagues had ever read Hosea, they would have told me that God(dess) is teaching Hosea to hate the sin, and love the sinner. Perhaps they would even tell me that the command in Hosea 3:3 for Gomer to give up her career as a sex worker is similar to God(dess)'s call for me to stop being gay. Or, they may just shrug it all off as a metaphor. Of course Hosea is a metaphor of God(dess)'s relationship with Israel, but it is still a queer metaphor!

Many queer commentators of the Hebrew Bible have shown that YHVH can be described as queer and/or transgender, and an anally raping phallocentric God(dess) who is not only David's top but the Top of all Tops. [152] Ken Stone's queer commentary on Hosea also uncovers a queer YHVH that transgresses heterosexual norms that contribute masculinity to men.[153] Stone argues that though Hosea is a phallocentric text, that Hosea is emasculated when he takes a whore as his wife. Hosea is emasculated further when only Gomer's first born is identified specifically as his offspring, leaving the paternity of the other two children in question.[154] While Stone's queer commentary highlights the feminine traits displayed by the male YHVH (queer gender expression), he stops short of calling YHVH erotically queer (queer sexual expression).

YHVH's Same-Sex Vows

Because Hosea is writing in the style of poetry, tragedy and comedy, it is unlikely that the story in the opening chapters of Hosea is biographical.[155] While Hosea's domestic relations may be accurately portrayed, the children in this book have names that express a relationship to God(dess) that change at God(dess)'s discretion. Thus, it is more likely that this text uses Hosea's family as a way to show Israel's relationship to YHVH rather than Hosea's historical realty.[156]

Though it is given less attention than the relationship between Hosea and Gomer, I believe that the relationship between God(dess) and Gomer's third born son is actually the central relationship in the text. The author of Hosea 2 shows the reader the importance of Gomer's third born son by referencing him at the beginning and ending of the story. Also, it is only in the renaming of Gomer's third son from "Not my People," to "You are

---

[152] See Theodore W. Jennings, Jr., "YHVH as Erastes;" and Roland Boer, "Yahweh as Top: A Lost Targum," in Queer Commentary and the Hebrew Bible.

[153] Stone cautions that this is not a complete transgression, because there women are not liberated from the phallocentric understandings in this text (Lovers and Raisin Cakes, 139). See Stone, Ken, "Lovers and Raisin Cakes: Food, Sex and Divine Insecurity in Hosea," Queer Commentary and the Hebrew Bible, and Stone, Ken, Practicing Safer Texts, 207-239.

[154] "Lovers and Raisin Cakes," 134-135.

[155] Buss, Martin J., "Tragedy and Comedy in Hosea," Semeia, No. 32, 1984, p. 71; and Morris, Gerald, Prophecy, Poetry and Hosea, Sheffield Academic Press, 1996, 42.

[156] Light, Gary, W., "The New Covenant in the Book of Hosea," Review & Expositor, 90, Spring, 1993, 222.

my People," by God(dess) that the entire text can be understood and specifically what happens to Gomer and Hosea.

It is in the dramatic ending of the text in 2:23, where YHVH says to "Not-My-People," "You are My-People" that the marriage vows in 2:16 between Hosea and Gomer became a means of reconciliation for YHVH and Israel.[157] Gary Light calls the transformation of the third child into "You are My People" and the third child's response "(You are) my God" as another exchange of vows that brings an "intimate, personal relationship with [God(dess)] that goes far beyond a legal contract."[158] Are these vows marriage vows? The fact that marriage vows are mentioned twice (2:19-20) in the verses that precede the vows between YHVH and Gomer's third born indicates that the vows are about betrothal.

Queer readers may be more inclined to see the proclamations "You are my People" and "You are my God" as a marriage vow because of the similarity to the vows made between Ruth and Naomi (Ruth 1:16-17):

> But Ruth said, "Entreat me not to leave you or to return from following you; for where you go I will go, and where you lodge I will lodge; *your people shall be my people, and your God my God*; where you die I will die, and there I will be buried. May the Lord do so to me and more also if even death parts me from you.[159]

The vows in Ruth, "Your people shall be my people" and "your God my God" echo the vows in Hosea "You are my People" and "You are my God." The vows in Ruth are often dismissed by contemporary Western readers who believe that wedding vows are only legitimate if they reflect their monogamous understanding of marriage (even though polyamorus and biligomous relationships often appear in the Hebrew Bible). The Ruth text is often dismissed as a wedding vow because Ruth goes on to seduce Boaz, at Naomi's suggestion, and conceive David. Ironically, though straight readers rarely view the Ruth text as a wedding between Ruth and Naomi,

---

[157] Light, 228-229

[158] Light, 228-229.

[159] Revised Standard Version.

the Ruth text is used more than any other in contemporary straight wedding ceremonies.

And while the existence of polyamory in the Ruth text may be enough to prove Ruth's heterosexuality to a straight audience, queer readers may see a parallel to the plight of the many queer individuals throughout history who have married a member of the opposite sex because of their own inner homophobia, to escape persecution and/or to conceive a child. In 1 Samuel chapters 18-21 a similar scenario plays out between David and Jonathon where the two men declare that they will love each other the best, though David later marries many women and has inappropriate sexual relationships with others.

Just as straight readers have missed and/or denied the queer wedding vows in Ruth, they are also missing the queer wedding that takes place in Hosea 2. Commentators are quick to argue that YHVH's relationship to the third born son gives meaning to the relationship between Hosea and Gomer, but they fail to let Hosea and Gomer's relationship give meaning to the relationship established between the third born son and YHVH. If they were to do this they would have to recognize the vows between YHVH and the third born son as marriage vows. The text identifies Hosea as a male, calling him "son of Beeri" (1:1) who has marriage vows with a woman, called "Gomer the daughter of Dibliam" (1:3). The wedding that takes place between Hosea and Gomer is between a man and a woman. YHVH, a masculine word in the Hebrew, marries the third born who is a son (1:8). The marriage between YHVH and the third born is between a man and a man.

I am not surprised that most commentators have not seen YHVH as queer, but I am surprised that the author of Hosea chose to represent YHVH as queer despite his position in society. As Edward Campbell, Jr writes: "Amos and Hosea are better seen not as themselves downtrodden and thus protesting 'from below,' but as informed and empathic observers from the ranks of the well-to-do, indignant at the effects of the unfolding social and economic structure."[160] I would expect to find a queer YHVH in the text of a marginalized person, just as people are likely to read this and say

---

[160] Campbell, Edward F., Jr, "A Land Divided: Judah and Israel from the Death of Solomon to the Fall of Samaria," The Oxford History of the Biblical World, 235.

that I am only discovering that YHVH is queer, because I am queer and I want YHVH to be like me. So why does the well to do author of this text include a queer YHVH? Because this text shows to its audience, the sons of Israel, that YHVH is their master and the master of their enemies' gods.

I believe the wedding vows between YHVH and the third born son is a direct reference and proper analogy to the identified audience in the text: the sons of Israel (4:1). Just as Hosea marries Gomer who represents Israel,[161] YHVH marries the third born son of Gomer or the sons of Israel. This interpretation of the text, is consistent with the explanation within Hosea: "And YHVH said to me, 'Go again [Hosea], love a woman who is beloved of a paramour and is an adultress; even as YHVH loves the sons of Israel, though they turn to other Gods and love cakes and raisins'" (3:1). YHVH's relationship with the sons of Israel is also alluded to in later verses in chapter 3. Each time Hosea speaks to Gomer it is followed by a parallel response about how YHVH interacts with the sons of Israel. When Hosea tells Gomer she will not play the harlot (3:3) then YHVH leaves the sons of Israel without a king or prince and they return to YHVH (3:4-5).

Sexual mores of the time would indicate that the marriage between YHVH and the son of Israel/Gomer is not a marriage between equals but that YHVH is the master of the son(s) of Israel. At the time that Hosea was written, the passive partner in the sex act is seen as subordinate and is probably the slave of the active male partner. This description of YHVH as the master is consistent with Roland Boer's understanding of YHWH as a top.[162] Theodore Jennings, Jr's examination of the similarities between the 1 Samuel story of David, Saul and Jonathon with the story of Erastes, shows how Israelites used the popular myths of their enemies to show that YHVH is the Top of all Tops and thus the God above their enemy's gods.[163] In Hosea 2, YHVH can also be seen as the Top of all Tops without altering or manipulating the text.

---

[161] It is nearly a universal understanding that Gomer is analogous to Israel Hosea 4 also seems to validate this understanding.: see Deroche, Michael, "The Reversal of Creation in Hosea."

[162] Boer, "Yahweh as Top: A Lost Targum.

[163] See Jennings, Jr., Theodore W., "YHVH as Erastes."

YHVH's Homoeroticism

Does YHVH consummate this marriage with the third born child? If it is true, as I have argued above, that the power of having YHVH marry the third born comes from the Israelites ability to show that YHVH is the Top of all Tops, then YHVH must consummate his marriage with the third born son. In addition to the rhetorical affect, sex and sexuality pervades the Hosea text. Renita Weems argues:

> Not only have scholars neglected the peculiarly literary character of the material in Hosea, they have also failed to consider in any substantial way the significance of Hosea's use of sexual imagery and gynomorphic language to describe the volatile character of the divine-human relationship... For what was the case in ancient Israel remains the case in modern times: talk about sex and sexuality tends to provoke, rouse, humiliate, and captivate people.[164]

It would be out of the ordinary for YHVH not to consummate his marriage in a text that is so thoroughly wrapped up in sex and sexual innuendo.

Not only is it improbable, but I believe there are also clues within the text that encourage the reader to see that YHVH engages in sexual activity with men. Scholars working from a heterocentric mindset have failed to acknowledge what is present in the text, even when they notice that their interpretations of the text do not match what they find in the text. Several scholars note that there is a strange gender play going on in Hosea. Weems writes: "In a book such as Hosea where pronouns can change from one verse to another, themes are erratic, and, compared to other prophetic books, the oracular formula is rarely found, there is considerable diversity among scholars about how to divide up the poems."[165] Scholars have not only noted the changes in gender pronouns, they also participate in changing them, to create a text that more accurately illustrates their interpretations.[166]

---

[164] Weems, 89.

[165] Weems, 93.

However, one element remains unchanged by the author, editors and commentators that shows the homoerotic nature of YHVH. Biblical scholars and theologians have long noted the use of agricultural imagery in talking about fertility.[167] Contemporary audiences also use sayings such as "planting his seed" and "sowing his oats" in a similar manner. "Sowing" has traditionally been understood as sexual in a world that views "human women as soil, waiting for the sowing of male seed."[168] Hosea's first born son is called "Jezreel" which literally means "God sows."[169] Could this mean God sows the women and produces the sons of Israel? Yes, in fact this is the interpretation that most scholars have come to. However, I believe that it is also possible (and more appropriate according to my previous arguments) to argue that YHVH sows the sons of Israel. My interpretation is also supported by the text: "and they shall answer Jezreel; and I will sow him for myself in the land (2:22-23).

While it would be unlikely that YHVH failed to consummate his marriage with the third born son of Gomer/Israel, the text both alludes to and explicitly states that YHVH sows the

---

[166] Ken Stone, in his queer commentary on Hosea, also notes the strange gender play and even argues that purposeful mistranslations are one method that has been used to make sense of the text. Stone argues that in Hosea 2:23 "I will sow her" is replaced with "him" with "no textual warrant for the substitution." ["Lovers and Raisin Cakes," 134.] The gender of the male form of the word flax was changed to the female form in Massoretic text because "nowhere else in the Old Testament does a masculine singular form of the word in question occur. The word for 'flax' in biblical Hebrew belongs to a large class of nouns that have feminine form in singular and masculine form in plural..." [Tangberg, K A., "Note on pisti in Hosea 2:7,11." Vestus testamentum, 27 No. 2, April, 1977, p. 222.]

[167] See "Lovers and Raisin Cakes" for a more thorough examination of this topic. Also, this connection of fertility and argricultureal planting seems to be confirmed by archealogical findings. Like the skeleton in an early Copper Age grave from Varna, Bulgaria: "The Varna skeleton seems to have been buried face-down in the earth, with penis erect, as if fertilizing the soil; and I wonder whether this object could have been used in a fertility ritual similar to one known from the ethnographic record of North America, in which a transexual of the Zuni people was publicly masturbated in the spring to ensure the return of wildlife." [Taylor, Timothy, "Uncovering the Prehistory of Sex" British Archaeology, No. 15, June 1996, Electronically Recovered on 8/15/2005 (http://www.britarch.ac.uk/ba/ba15/ba15feat.html).]

[168] Ibid, 134.

[169] Ibid, 134.

first born son of Israel. The author of Hosea chooses to portray YHVH as the Top of all Tops that exchanges same-sex marriage vows with and engages in homoerotic behavior with the sons of Israel.

Word Alone Calls Lutherans to Ordain Non-Celibate GLBTQ Individuals

The Living Word of the Gospel: Jesus, Demons and the Call to "Go and Do Likewise"

Demonic Disciples, Prophets and Preachers in the Gospel of Mark

The oldest testament of Jesus, the Gospel of Mark is so provocative that many scholars believe the other Gospels were written to make the story more comfortable for audiences.[170] The first corrections were added to Mark itself, you may have noticed that in the sixteenth chapter of Mark there are several endings listed. The first and oldest ending is verse 16:8, where the women at the tomb say "nothing to no one for they were afraid." This strange ending is a catalyst to force those who hear the story of Jesus to be the only ones able to share the Good News. While highly affective, it is a very uncomfortable ending.

In Mark's Gospel, nothing happens that is expected, and it is certainly not the Gospel story that gets portrayed in movies and musicals about Jesus. First, there is no nativity, no donkey, no magi, no shepherds, no menagerie, and no babies. In a dramatically Lutheran way, this story of Jesus begins with his baptism. But this is no typical baptism, since the heavens were literally torn in two (1:10).

You may remember in the first creation story that God(dess) puts a dome over the earth (Genesis 1:6), that separates the water/rain, swirling chaos, the stuff of God(dess) and the stuff

---

[170] Many of my learning's about the Gospel of Mark came from my many classes taught by Rev. Dr. Richard Swanson and Dr. Mary Tolbert. For those who may not have the good graces to attend their classes, I recommend: Tolbert, Sowing the Gospel; and Swanson, Richard W., Provoking the Gospel of Mark: A Storyteller's Commentary Year B, Pilgrim Press, 2005.

of demons from the earth and the stuff of humans. In the story of Noah, it begins to rain when the windows of the dome of heaven are opened, letting the water fall to the earth (Genesis 7:11; 8:2).

When the heavens are torn in two at Jesus' baptism, not only is the Holy Spirit in the form of a dove able to descend down to earth, but all the demons are able to come down too along with water (which could explain all the storms on the sea). What an exciting way to begin a story. Can you imagine all the water, demons and stuff of God(dess) pouring out of the tear in the dome of heaven? It was probably as motley and chaotic as all the animals trying to get off of Noah's ark after the storm was over. I bet it was not as orderly as the two by two line that got them on the boat.

When everything pours out of heaven and down to earth and something descends into Jesus, the characters of the story do not know if it is the stuff of God(dess) or the stuff of demons that has gone into Jesus. This is why everyone in the story keeps remarking about how the demons listen to Jesus, they are trying to figure out if Jesus is a demon too. Jesus confronts the idea that he is a demon when his family comes to restrain him and take him home believing that he is a crazy demoniac (3:20-30). Instead of denying the allegations, Jesus disowns his family and proclaims that "whoever does the will of God(dess) is my brother and sister and mother."

Perhaps the experience of having his family think he is a demon helps Jesus to see through pietistic ritual, to sit with the tax collectors, sex workers and sinners and see that they are able to do the will of God(dess) despite the fact that they are not doing what is expected of them. Perhaps this makes it easier to be around smelly fisherman, gender bending male water carriers, a beautiful naked male stranger, a crazy demoniac named Legion, a man clothed in camel hair who eats locusts and honey and the hoards of hungry people that are always pushing him into the sea.

The Gospel of Mark is nothing like what would be expected. The disciples (which in Greek literally translates "learners") never learn. The one time Peter does proclaim the truth, Jesus calls him Satan (8:33). The only ones, who do get it right, are the ones who should be the least able to proclaim the Good News. The demons are the only group that consistently proclaim that Jesus is the Messiah. The Centurion also proclaims that Jesus is the son of God (in exact echo of the words from heaven during Jesus' baptism) after Jesus dies (15:39), but it takes an earthquake and the cloth in the Temple's holy of holy to tear (echoing the tearing of the dome of heaven) for him to figure it out. A part of the political system that just caused Jesus' death, the Centurion is surely an unexpected proclaimer of the Good News. The first and oldest ending (16:8) ends with learners who deny Jesus and flee and the women who say nothing to no one. The literal translation of the Greek is even more striking: "and the women nothing, nothing, nothing."

The demons knew who Jesus was (though Jesus rarely let them speak because he wanted his identity to be a secret), and they were the only ones who consistently proclaimed Jesus' identity. Perhaps this helps Jesus to notice that people do not have to be a part of his group or follow any particular rules to proclaim his message. If people could think that Jesus the son of God(dess) was a demon, why would it bother Jesus if people thought those proclaiming his message were demons or believed by society to be queer?

Literally talking about human excrement, Jesus says "there is nothing outside a person that by going in can defile, but the things that come out are what defile" (7:14-23). Jesus goes on to say that it is your actions and how you treat people that matters (not ritual or rules of piety). It is your heart that matters. Jesus goes even further to say that people do not even have to be a part of his group or follow his rules to do good things in his name (9:38-41).

On the one hand, Lutherans embrace this same spirit of Jesus' message by proclaiming the priesthood of all believers. However, in our election of pastors to proclaim the Word and administer the sacraments, we have decided who is in and who is out. Most of our requirements are about how to embody the Good News and to love our neighbor. However the requirement for queer pastors and seminarians to remain celibate seems strangely out of place (especially since Luther so strongly proclaimed that requiring a vow of celibacy was against the gospel), since they are told that they should not love in the way that God(dess) created them to.

Why would we (Lutherans) do something so seemingly out of sync with Jesus' actions and proclamation that you do not have to follow society's rules, the rules of the church or even Jesus' rules in order to proclaim Christ's message? I believe the answer can be found in the Gospel of Mark.

After Jesus is baptized, he calls his disciples and the demons recognize him in the synagogue, Jesus goes to Simon's house (1:29-34). Jesus heals Simon's mother-in-law (who had a fever) and then she gets up to "serve" them. This sounds like a stereotypical man, coming into a house and expecting the woman to cook even when she is sick. Of course, it could also have been that Simon's mother-in-law wanted to cook out of her gratitude or because that is what grandmothers do. Regardless of the motivations of Simon's mother-in-law, it would be easy to say that Jesus is bit patriarchal.

However, what you may not know if you do not read the original Greek is that the problem is in the translation. The word that is translated "serve" is only translated "serve" when it is talking about women. When biblical translators translate the exact same word when it is describing men, they translate it "minister." Why? Because, contemporary voices decided that women could not minister, and men would not serve. The Greek word is the root word for "deacon." This makes more sense in the text, where the very next verse does not describe the meal that was served, but rather talks about all the people that were brought to Jesus to be healed (which is exactly what we would expect a deacon to do).

It would be easy to say that Jesus was patriarchal, when all along it was our contemporary society that translated the words that way. We are patriarchal and so our bible is too. In the same way, we have written our homophobia into the bible. We have decided that someone is our "other." We call them demons and write them into the text saying that they are not worthy of God(dess)'s promise or to proclaim Christ's message. Ironically, the story of Simon's mother-in-law ends with Jesus again telling the demons not to speak because "they knew him" (1:34).

The Good News of the Gospel of Mark is that even those we label as demons can proclaim Christ's message and they may even be the only ones who will do it. When we are labeled as demons, we are still able to proclaim Christ's message and our focus should be on loving our neighbor and doing God(dess)'s will rather than on following the rules of the church, for whomever does the will of God(dess) is Christ's brother and sister and mother. So which character in the Gospel of Mark would you like to be? Would you like to be called a demon, but consistently proclaim the truth about God? Or, would you rather nothing, nothing, nothing?

The Good Samaritan (Luke 10:25-37)

The story of the Good Samaritan is one of the most memorable stories of the Greek Bible, and it was likely a very well known story before Jesus told it. What would have been surprising to Jesus' audience is that instead of having the average faithful Judean be the one who shows kindness to the stranger, he inserts a Samaritan in the story. To a Jew at the time of Jesus, Samaritan's were the most rejected outsiders who were considered rejecters of God(dess). Even more shocking is that Jesus tells the pious Jew to "go and do likewise." Go and be like a rejecter of God(dess)? Why wouldn't Jesus tell the lawyer to hate the sin, but love the sinner? But Jesus does not even mention the sinfulness or uncleanness of the Samaritan. The sinfulness of the Samaritan was so well known, that Jesus would not have needed to mention it; this is why the story works.

Richard Cleaver retells this story, but instead of a Samaritan, he casts the part with a gay man who is kicked out of the church after he testifies against the gay-bashers that killed his beloved:

> Suddenly he noticed what looked like a body beside the road. Stopping the car, he jumped out and rushed to look. A naked man, covered with blood and bruises. They looked a lot like the ones he had seen on Adam's body when he had found him in the alley outside their building. Obviously, this man too had been mugged, and judging from the fact that the muggers took all his clothes, the gay man figured it couldn't have been a simple robbery. He felt for a pulse: the man was still alive. Adam had not been; there had been nothing left to do for him. He was

being given a chance to make up now for his helplessness then.[171]

After helping the man, the newspapers pick up the story and the same bishop that had passed the man by on the road without helping him decides to give the gay man the Good Samaritan award. At the end of the Bishops long presentation, the gay man proclaims: "Oh, I didn't do it for religious reasons. It just seemed like the human thing to do. I haven't been to church since my priest refused me absolution when I confessed I was in love with the redheaded guy who was captain of the wrestling team."[172]

Cleaver's retelling of this story is poignant because some contemporary Christians see queer folk as people who have rejected God(dess), in the same way that the Jews believed the Samaritans had. Indeed, Jesus told the parable of the good Samaritan in an unconventional manner, Cleaver further suggests that Jesus is telling us "that it is to the oppressed, the heretic, the bugger that we must go for teaching rather than resting in the conventional pieties dispensed by the usual professionals?"[173]

How does this apply to the queer Lutheran pastors that are serving the church? Well our Bishops have declared that "homosexual sexual relationships" are sinful, have called for queer clergy and seminarians to abstain from their "sin" and remain celibate. I imagine that Jesus would see the faithful witness of the queer clergy and seminarians. I believe Jesus would notice the ways queer Lutherans work for justice, comfort the sick and serve those considered the "least" in society without the official recognition of church leaders. Jesus would tell the Bishops to "go and do likewise."

---

[171] Cleaver, Richard, Know My Name: A Gay Liberation Theology, Westminster John Knox Press, Louisville, Kentucky, 1995, 6.

[172] Ibid, 7.

[173] Ibid.

The Word of Paul: Exegesis of 1 Corinthians 7:17-40

Only, let every one lead the life which the Lord has assigned to [them], and in which God has called [them]. This is my rule in all the churches.

(1 Cor. 7:17 RSV).

Textual Context

Who are the Corinthians? Destroyed by the Romans in 146 BC, and rebuilt 100 years later, the community of Corinth included a "hotchpotch of races"[174] consisting first of the "freed slaves from Rome, but soon more people from east and west flocked there bringing a variety of beliefs and attitudes with them. Making them prone to form factions (cf. 1 Cor. 1:11f and 1 Clement, c. AD 96)."[175] It was known to ancient communities that "'to live like a Corinthian' meant to be sexually lax, lascivious."[176]

Due to Hellenistic influence, the residents of Corinth (and, as I will argue later, Paul) had three types of socially accepted norms for sexual encounters: "1. marriage, 2. fornication (casual, non-committal sex or prostitution), and 3. a love-relationship (partnership based on mutual love) without the formal ties involved in a marriage contract."[177] *Contemporary readers should take particular note that the gender of the sexual partner is not a factor in ancient times. Though some contemporary readers may suggest that no distinction is made because sex only occurred between a man and a woman this not only is unhistorical, it is also contrary to Paul's own mentioning of homoerotism in the beginning of Romans.*

Is Paul as liberal about sex as Hellenistic and Corinth society? Paul explicitly wants to be seen as different then other

---

[174] Molvaer, Reidulf K., "St Paul's Views on Sex According to 1 Corinthians 7:9 & 36-38," Studia Theologica, 58, 2004, 48.

[175] Ibid, 56.

[176] Ibid, 45.

[177] Ibid, 50.

Greeks. Paul creates distance between himself and other Greek scholars in the beginning of 1 Corinthians by arguing that the Greeks rely on wisdom, while Paul relies on the "foolishness" of God(dess).[178] However, despite Paul's desire to separate himself from other Greek writers, Paul's understanding of marriage is still in line with that of the Greek stoics (Musonius, Antipater, Epictetus & Hierocles).[179]

Even with his stoic understanding of the world, Paul still presents the same Hellenistic understanding that addresses all three types of sexual encounters mentioned above in 1 Corinthians. Despite contemporary belief that the bible only condones sex within marriage, Paul does not condemn pre-marital sexual relationships: "to have sex before marriage is thus not in itself condemned, it is no sin ('there is nothing wrong in it', NEB), no more than sex between true lovers who have been married before, but not to each other, v. 9. But abstinence is 'better', v. 38."[180]

Those who are looking to 1 Corinthians to find *vision and expectations* to rule the sex lives of the faithful, miss Paul's point: "For Paul, the impending wrap up of history is so vivid that it infuses all current questions, problems, dilemmas and challenges. If indeed the present form of the world is passing, he seems to reason, why waste energy on lesser orders of concern, such as slavery and sex?"[181] But, with the delay of the perousia, contemporary Christians have become just as obsessed with sex as the Corinth community was. In particular, the Lutheran church seems to have a surplus of time, money and energy to deal with issues of sex and sexuality. The remainder of this chapter will look at how 1 Cor. 7:17-40 can speak to the Lutheran church's position on the ordination of queer individuals.

1 Corinthians 7:17-40

---

[178] Welborn, Laurence L., "Μωρος γενεσθω: Paul's Appropriation of the Role of the Fool in 1 Corinthians 1-4" Biblical Interpretation, 10.4, 2002, 420-35.

[179] Balch, David L., "1 Cor. 7:32-35 and Stoic Debates about Marriage, Anxiety and Distraction." Journal of Biblical Liturature, 102/3, 1983, 429-39.

[180] Molvaer, "St Paul's Views on Sex According to 1 Corinthians 7:9 & 36-38," 54.

[181] Keim, Paul "Mutant ministry," Christian Century; Vol. 120 Issue 1, January 11, 2003, p17.

1 Corinthians 7:17-40, is the end of the second of five sections of Corinthians: "1) the cross, leadership and unity 1:4-4:16; 2) sex (men and women in the human family) 4:17-7:40; 3) idols (Christian and non-Christian) 8-11:1; 4) worship, gifts and love (men and women in worship) 11:2-14; and 5) the resurrection 15."[182] Despite the fact that the majority of the section deals with sex, recent academic focus on 1 Cor. 7:17-40 has predominantly been on verses 7:21-22 and its implications for slaves.[183] Rightly, slavery has been the focus of scholarship because of the emotional and psychological memories of the colonial slavery and the lasting power of the African-American civil rights movement. However though simultaneously markedly different and disappointingly similar to colonial slavery, the queer civil rights movement may have similar emotional and psychological memories for future generations. Can this text accurately speak to the issues of queer individuals and communities today? I believe it can speak specifically to the ordination of non-celibate queer individuals in the Lutheran church.

1 Cor. 7:17-40 has regularly been used by major church monastics and scholars to talk about the role of celibacy in monastic life. Augustine, Jerome, and Ambrosiaster have used this text from Paul to support the "superiority of celibacy to marriage."[184] During the Reformation, theologians began to move away from this understanding of the supremacy of celibacy. This movement is seen first in the work of Erasmus (even before the Reformation), then with Melancthon (in 1522) and finally in the anticlerical writings of Martin Luther (1523).[185] Luther's main support for his understanding that the call to ministry and the call to celibacy were

---

[182] Baily, Kenneth, E., "The Structure of I Corinthians and Paul's Theological Method with Special Reference to 4:17," Novum Testamentum, XXV, 2, 1963, 154.

[183] There are those arguing that this passages relieves slaves from their masters: Deming, Will, "A Diatribe Pattern in 1 Cor 7:21-22 : A New Perspective on Paul's Directions to Slaves," Novum testamentum, 37, April 1995, p 130-137. And those who argue that this passage calls everyone to be a slave: Willson, Patrick J, "The freedom of slavery : 1 Cor 9:16-23;" Christian Century, 111 Jan 19, 1994, p 43.

[184] Thompson, John L., "Apostolic Doctrine and Apostolic Advice in 1 Corinthians 7," 1992 Annual Meeting of the American Society of Church History in Washington D.C., December 29, 1992, 4, Electronically Retrieved, EBCOHOST, 3-6.

[185] Ibid, 9-12.

two separate calls comes from his interpretation of 1 Cor 7:17-40.[186]
For Luther, requiring priests to be celibate was against the gospel.[187]

So why does the Lutheran church continue to require celibacy for queer individuals who are "homosexual in their self-understanding"? The Word Alone organization, who is one of the most vocal groups in the Lutheran church against the ordination of queer individuals (regardless of their willingness to be celibate), is ironically also the same group that is one of the most vocal proponents of the priesthood of ALL believers. Word Alone is against the ordination of queer individuals because they believe that being queer is sinful. They even encourage queer individuals to become a part of Exodus International to be "set free from homosexual behavior"[188]

I believe that it is possible to argue that "homosexual behavior" is not sinful through exegesis of the six passages that have been the primary concern of contemporary bible study on homosexuality. I also believe that it is possible to show the flawed logic of current ELCA policy and Word Alone by continuing to look at the 1 Cor. text.

Let's imagine for a moment that Word Alone is correct in arguing that homosexuality is sinful. As a Lutheran community that has historically believed that we are all equal in our sinfulness, is homoerotism something that should prevent people from ordained ministry? Can a sinful person be called to ordained ministry? In his exegesis of 1 Corinthians, Luther speaks directly to this question:

> But what if the Gospel calls me in a state of sin, should I remain in that? Answer: **If you have entered into faith and love, that is, if you are in the call of the Gospel, then sin as much as you please.** But how can you sin if you have faith and love? Since God is satisfied with your faith and your neighbor with your love, it is impossible that you should be called and still remain in a state of sin. If, however, you remain in that state, then either you were not called as yet, or you did not comprehend the call. For this call brings you from the

---

[186] See Chapter 4.

[187] Luther, "The Judgment of Marin Luther on Monastic Vows".

[188] http://www.wordalone.org/resources/index.html

state of sin to a state of virtue, making you unable to sin as long as you are in that state. All things are free to you with God through faith; but with men you are the servant of everyman through love.

From this you will see that monasticizing and making of spiritual regulations is all wrong in our time. For these people bind themselves before God to outward things from which God has made them free, thus working against the freedom of faith and God's order.[189]

Here, Luther is speaking directly about the matter of celibacy and the priesthood. It would seem that the only question that would remain for Luther is: Is homoeroticism a sign of faith and love? As we have discussed earlier, Paul's Hellenistic understanding of the three types of sexual encounters did not make a distinction between same-sex and opposite-sex sexual relations. Additionally, Paul argues that it is not bad to have sex outside of marriage (though abstinence is better). But was homoeroticism an act of love and faith for Luther? Homoeroticism existed in Luther's day, yet in all of his writings Luther only mentions homosexuality one time. While Luther does condemn male effeminacy, he does not condemn all homosexuality. Instead, he condemns "excessive passion from shameful thoughts, through rubbing with hands, through fondling of another's body, especially a woman's, through indecent movements, etc"[190] that occurs in BOTH homosexual and heterosexual intercourse. For Luther, the problem with these types of intercourse is that they are individual rather than partner oriented. Does this mean that Luther supports homoeroticism that is between two partner-oriented individuals? Like Jesus, Luther's lack of condemnation must be seen as support, for if Luther had an opinion about it he would have written about it – as Luther was not one to hold back an opinion.[191]

---

[189] LW28: *1 Corinthians 7, 1 Corinthians 15, Lectures on 1 Timothy.*

[190] LW25: *Lectures on Romans.*

[191] Though many Lutherans wish that Luther would have kept his opinions on the place of a woman and the Jews to himself.

Finding nothing to condemn or support homosexuality in Luther's writing, imagine for a moment that Luther did believe homoeroticism was a sin, as Word Alone argues. In the same way that Paul urges us not to spend so much time worrying about matters of sex and sexuality, Luther argues the same (in words strikingly similar to his comments on the 1 Cor. passage) in his famous word to Philip Melancthon:

> **Be a sinner and sin☐☐ boldly,☐☐ but believe and☐[34]☐ rejoice in Christ even more boldly, for he is victorious over sin, death, and the world. As long as we are here [in this world]☐☐ we have to sin.** This life is not the dwelling place of righteousness,☐[36]☐ but, as Peter says,☐ we look for new heavens and a new earth in which righteousness☐ dwells. It is enough that by☐[39]☐ the riches of God's glory we have come to know the Lamb that takes away the sin of the world.☐[40]☐ **No sin will separate us from the Lamb, even though we commit fornication and murder a thousand times a day.** [192]

Our Lutheran heritage, tradition and confessions call us to remember Christ's saving action, God(dess)'s transforming grace and our baptismal call to the priesthood of all believers regardless of our sinfulness, social-economic status, education or sexuality. We are called by Paul and Luther to focus on the call of an individual, not their sexuality. If we truly want the word alone (*sola scriptura*) to guide us in our decision to ordain queer individuals, then we need to remember the words of 1 Cor. 7:17-40.

Only, let every one lead the life which the Lord has assigned to [them], and in which God(dess) has called [them]. This is my rule in all the churches. (1 Cor. 7:17 RSV).

---

[192] LW48: *Letters I.*

Conclusion

We are like [people] who read the sign posts and never travel the road they indicate.
-Martin Luther[193]

As Lutherans we boldly proclaim that in our baptisms we are washed clean of our sin. Baptized as babies we proudly proclaim that God(dess) names and claims us before we have the ability to accept or deny God(dess). The waters of baptism liberate us from our sin so that we can "sin boldly and believe more boldly still,"[194] because nothing can separate us from the love of God(dess). But do we *really* believe that baptism cleanses all people of their sins? If we truly believed all the things we proclaim, Lutherans would be able to boldly affirm the baptismal call of queer Lutherans.

As Lutherans we proclaim a priesthood of all believers and that the call to celibacy and the call to the priesthood are separate call. We proclaim this so strongly that our book of confessions state that to require priests to be celibate is against the gospel. Our confessions even have an extraordinary process in place to be used to ordain priests when bishops go against the gospel and try to require celibacy (the same extraordinary process that some Extraordinary Lutherans[195] follow in their ordinations – including mine). But do we *really* believe that the call to celibacy is a separate call from the call to ordained ministry? If we truly believed all the things we proclaim, Lutherans would proudly ordain queer individuals who are non-celibate and apologize for the harm that has been caused to families, individuals and communities that have required queer individuals to be celibate, in the closet, or non-queer.

---

[193] LW44: *The Christian in Society I : To the Christian Nobility of the German Nation Concerning the Reform of the Christian Estate.*

[194] LW48: 91 To Phillip Melanchthon, Wartburg, August 1, 1521.

[195] See Extraordinary Lutheran Ministry, www.elm.org

As Lutherans we proclaim that all people are equal in their sinfulness and that all people exist simultaneously as both saint and sinner. But do we *really* believe that all people are equally sinful? If we truly believed all the things we proclaim, Lutherans would be able to boldly affirm that queer Lutherans are equal to non-queer Lutherans and apologize for making them objects of countless studies, votes and policies.

> *This church, in faithfulness to the Gospel, is committed to be an inclusive church in the midst of division in society. Therefore, in their organization and outreach, the congregations, synods, and churchwide units of this church shall seek to exhibit the inclusive unity that is God's will for the Church.* —ELCA Constitution[196]

---

[196] November 12, 2005 version.

Appendix

Extraordinary Prayer Calendar[197]

A celebration of queer saints (living and passed) that do not always make it onto the prayer cycles in Lutheran Churches.

"THIS is, I think, a queer and odd saint..." – Martin Luther on Jonah[198]

January 1991: Ordination of Pastor Jenny Mason: The Rev. Dr. Jenny Mason, a member of the Extraordinary Lutheran Ministries roster, served as an ELCA missionary in Santiago, Chile before being removed from the ELCA clergy roster in 2001 for being an openly lesbian woman in relationship. More recently, Jenny served as Associate Pastor at Central City Lutheran Mission (CCLM) in San Bernardino, California. CCLM provides ministry, housing and support services to the inner city poor, homeless, people of color, and those living with HIV in inland Southern California. CCLM was disciplined by the Synod for installing Jenny as an openly lesbian woman pastor, resulting in the loss of both funding and their official ELCA status. She holds a Master of Divinity degree from Trinity Lutheran Seminary in Columbus, OH, and a Doctorate of Ministry in Proclamation from the Lutheran School of Theology, Chicago. She is married to Pastor Jodi Barry, who is also on the Extraordinary Lutheran Ministries roster (see October 25).

---

[197] Primary sources for this section includes: Boswell, John, Same-Sex Unions in Premodern Europe, Villard Books, 1994; Hotchkiss, Clothes Make the Man.; Cloke, This Female Man of God.; Omingender; Cassell's Encyclopedia; and the biographies written about members of the Extraordinary Lutheran Ministries (ELM) roster posted online (as of May 2009) at www.elm.org. The ELM biographies were predominately compiled by Megan M. Rohrer, with additions and corrections submitted by the roster members and staff of ELM. Additional hagiography of many of the saints can be located by looking up the prayer calendar they are associated (listed with each of the recognized saints).

[198] LW19: *Minor Prophets II: Jonah and Habakkuk.*

January 1, 1999: Ordination of Pastor Robyn Hartwig: Pastor Robyn is dually rosterd by both the ELCA and Extraordinary Lutheran Ministries. Pastor Robyn received a MDiv from Pacific Lutheran Theological Seminary in 1997 and is currently working on ecology ministry in Oregon.

January 5: Feast day of St. Apollinaria/Dorotheos (According to the Orthodox Calendar)- Apollinaria/Dorotheos was a female born ascetic who wore male monastic habits. Apollinaria, also called Apollinaris Syncletica, left zir wealthy home in Rome to live the life of a hermit in the desert near Jerusalem. Zie then journeyed to the lavra of St. Macarius in Scete and, so disfigured was zie by zir ascetic life, that zie was thought to be a man and assumed the name of Dorotheos. Apollinaria/Dorotheos refused to identify as female even when zie was accused and condemned falsely of seduction and rape.

January 9: Feast day of SS. Polyeuctus and Nearchus, martyrs (According to Armenian Calendars)- Two early martyrs who were paired together by early Christians as a same-sex couple, and invoked as such in the "adelphopoiia" ceremonies. John Boswell argues that their ceremony provides historical proof of a Christian tradition of monogomous and publicly recognized same-sex unions.[199] St. Polyeuctus had a huge church, modeled after the Temple of Solomon, built in his name in 6th century Constantinople. Polyeuctus' final words to Nearchus are: "remember our secret vow."

January 12: Feast day of St. Aelred of Rievaulx, abbot (According to the Old Roman Calendar and the Episcopal Book of Common Prayers)- c.1110- 1167; One of the most lovable saints who was of noble birth, Aelred first lived at the court of David, Kind of Scotland. In 1135, at the age of twenty-six, Aelred entered the Cistercian abbey of Rievaulx. Ten years later he became abbot,

---

[199] See Boswell, John, Same-Sex Unions in Premodern Europe, Villard Books, 1994.

which he remained until his death in 1167. This monastery, where a great fervor and charity reigned, counted more than three hundred monks. Aelred who only sought "to love and to be loved", tasted pure happiness there whist making others happy and believed that the cross was the sign of the transgender Jesus' intimate invitation of embrace. Aelred also believed that Jesus' "naked breast will feed you."

St. Aelred writes: "It is no small consolation in this life to have someone you can unite with you in an intimate affection and the embrace of a holy love, someone in whom your spirit can rest, to whom you can pour out your soul, to whose pleasant exchanges, as to soothing songs, you can fly in sorrow... with whose spiritual kisses, as with remedial salves, you may draw out all the weariness of your restless anxieties. A man who can shed tears with you in your worries, be happy with you when things go well, search out with you the answers to your problems, whom with the ties of charity you can lead into the depths of your heart; ... where the sweetness of the Spirit flows between you, where you so join yourself and cleave to him that soul mingles with soul and two become one."

January 15, 2003: Censure of St. Paul-Reformation Lifted (see April 28)

January 19, 2008: Ordination of Pastor Jen Nagel in Minneapolis, Minnesota: Pastor Jen, a member of the Extraordinary Lutheran Ministries roster, was called to Salem Lutheran where she had been serving for four and a half years as a pastoral minister. Jen is trained in intentional interim ministry. She holds an M.Div. from University of Chicago-Divinity School, completed work at Lutheran School of Theology in Chicago and Concordia College, Moorhead Minnesota. She's served at Central Lutheran Church and Hennepin County Medical Center in Minneapolis, in Africa, Chicago, Michigan, and outdoor ministry settings. Jen has served as a member of the US Board of the World Council of Churches and on the Synod Council.

January 20, 1990: Ordination of Prs. Ruth Frost, Phyllis Zilhart, and Jeff Johnson: Pastors Ruth (see December 16), Phyllis (September 9) and Jeff (November 7) are members of the Extraordinary Lutheran Ministries roster and were ordained at the first extraordinary service at St. Paulus Lutheran Church in San Francisco that was attended by over 1000 persons, with participation by over 70 clergy members. The pastors were considered ineligible for placement in an ELCA congregation because of a denominational policy that requires a pledge of celibacy from gay and lesbian pastors.

January 20: Feast Day of St. Sebastian, martyr (According to both the New and Old Roman Calendar)- The martyrdom of St. Sebastian, about whom little is known, has been a subject for countless artists to portray the male body (see the front cover). St. Sebastian was killed by multiple arrow shots, an image of suffering and redemption which provided the basis for his cult. While St. Sebastian may not have been queer, there is a clear connection between the art of St. Sebastian and homoeroticism.

January 21: Feast Day of Agnes of Monçada- Lived for twenty years, disguised as a man, as a hermit in a cave near a monastery in Porta-coelia in order to avoid marriage and remain celibate.[200]

January 22, 1990: Charges filed against St. Francis and First United in San Francisco (see January 20)

January 25, 2008: Ordination of Pastor Steve Keiser at Lutheran Church of the Holy Communion in Philadelphia, Pennsylvania: Pastor Steve is a member of the Extraordinary Lutheran Ministries roster is a graduate of Wheaton College (1981, BA in Philosophy) and the Lutheran Theological Seminary at Philadelphia (1999, M.Div). Prior to entering seminary, he worked in branch management for fifteen years for Bell Savings Bank and Meridian Bank (now Wachovia). He has taught at Cabrini College, the

---

[200] Hotchkiss, 131.

Lutheran Seminary and for the Adventures Program at the seminary. He has also assisted Dr. Katie Day, a sociologist of religion who is studying the impact of volunteerism on churches burned as a result of arson. His ministry at Holy Communion includes working with young adults and establishing small group ministries.

February 3, 1998: Pastor Steve Sabin Expelled from ELCA Roster (see June 30)

February 11: Feast day of St. Euphrosyne/Smaragdus (According to the Old Roman Calendar; also celebrated on Sept 25 in the Orthodox Calendar)- Euphrosyne/Smaragdus was a female born ascetic who wore male monastic habits. Daughter of Paphnutius, a rich citizen of Alexandria, Egypt, born in zir parents' old age due to the prayers of a monk who was a friend of the family. When Euphrosyne was grown, the family arranged a marriage for zir to wealthy young noble, but zie preferred religious life. While Euphrosyne' father was on a retreat, zie gave away all possessions, and became a nun and spiritual student of the monk who'd prayed for zir birth. To hide from family, Euphrosyne/Smaragdus wore men's clothes, and became a monk, using the name Smaragdus. Smaragdus' beauty so distracted the other monks that the abbot ordered zir to live as a recluse in zir cell, however, Smaragdus became famous for holiness and wisdom, and became a spiritual teacher of zir father, who did not recognize zir. On Euphrosyne/Smaragdus deathbed zie revealed zir true identity to zir father who then became a monk, and lived in Euphrosyne/Smaragdus' cell the remaining ten years of his life.

February 12: Feast day of St. Mary/Marinos of Alexandria (According to the Orthodox Calendar)- Marina/os, unlike our other female born ascetics who wore male monastic habits, entered a convent as a tiny child with zir father who was concerned about Marina's fate if zie were left alone in the sinful world. He impressed upon Marina the importance of concealing zir true sex and zie assumed the name of Marinos. Years later zie was accused of fathering a child, still refusing to identify as female, zie lived outside of the monastery gate with the baby After five years, Marinos was allowed to return to the monastery where Marinos humbly lived a life of great hardship, while continuing to be a father to the child.

February 18, 2001: Ordination of Pastor Craig Minich: Craig Minich, a member of the Extraordinary Lutheran Ministries roster, was ordained as Pastor of Youth Ministries for the Oakland-Berkeley Lutheran Youth Program. Pastor Minich was called by three Evangelical Lutheran Church in America (ELCA) congregations — St. Paul Lutheran, Oakland, United Lutheran, Oakland, and University Lutheran Chapel, Berkeley.

Craig, a 1999 graduate of Pacific Lutheran Theological Seminary in Berkeley, California. Craig established the Oakland- Berkeley Youth Ministry in 1999 and served as a lay director until his ordination.

February 19, 1994: Pastor Ross Merkel's ELCA disciplinary hearing ends: Pastor Ross Merkel, is a member of the Extraordinary Lutheran Ministries roster and the current pastor of St. Paul Lutheran Church in Oakland, California. Ordained in 1978, he is a graduate of Lutheran Theological Southern Seminary in Columbia, South Carolina. Prior to being called to St. Paul in 1982, Pastor Merkel served as a Refugee Resettlement Coordinator with Lutheran Social Services of the Southwest in Phoenix, Arizona and prior to that as Associate Pastor of Grace Lutheran Church, Phoenix.

A native Californian, he graduated from the University of California, Davis with a Bachelor of Arts and then attended Brigham Young University in Provo, UT where he earned a Bachelor of Science and a Masters of Library Science.

February 19: Birthday of Greg Egertson: Greg, member of the Extraordinary Lutheran Ministries roster, is the oldest of six sons, his parents are the Rev. Dr. Paul W. Egertson (Bishop Emeritus, Southern California West Synod ELCA) and Shirley Smith Egertson. He was raised in the American Lutheran Church and comes from a family of Lutheran pastors, including his father, grandfather and brother.

Greg graduated from California Lutheran University in 1978 with a bachelor's degree in Psychology. Two years later, he completed the requirements for an undergraduate degree in Music. He worked at UCLA as a Research Associate in the Neuropsychiatric Institute until 1982, when he relocated to San Francisco. Since then, he has been a member at St. Francis Lutheran Church where has served in a number of leadership roles, including congregation president.

In 1983 Greg enrolled as an openly gay student at Pacific Lutheran Theological Seminary (PLTS), in Berkeley, CA. Often referred to as the "fourth seminarian," Greg was a classmate of Jeff Johnson, Jim Lancaster and Joel Workin, "the Berkeley three." After completing his internship at St. James Lutheran Church in Portland, Oregon, Greg graduated from PLTS in 1989. Because he refused to vow celibacy, Greg was not approved for ordination in the ELCA. Upon his return to San Francisco, Greg was appointed to serve on the call committee at St. Francis that called Ruth Frost and Phyllis Zillhart to serve with Jeff Johnson as the founding pastors of Lutheran Lesbian & Gay Ministries (LLGM).

In 1993, Greg became a founding board member of the Extraordinary Candidacy Project (ECP) where he served until 2003. He joined the LLGM Board in 1998 and was approved for ordination by the ECP in 1999. During his time with LLGM, Greg filled many board positions including co-chair. He helped to shepherd several extraordinary ordinations and installations of ECP pastors. He also provided key leadership in the visioning process that resulted in a merger between LLGM and ECP that became Extraordinary Lutheran Ministries.

In his secular life, Greg currently holds a position as Associate Dean for Budget, Administration and Enrollment Management at Golden Gate University School of Law in San Francisco.

February 20, 2005: Trinity Lutheran Church in Alameda Installs Pastor Craig Minich: (see February 18)

February 21: Death of Pope Julius II- 1443-1513; Born Giuliano della Rovere, Pope Julius II was thought to be homoerotically inclined. Despite evidence of a relationship with Lucrezia Normanni which led to the birth of a daughter, Felice, rumours surrounded Julius throughout his pontificate (and subsequently) about his same-sex desires. Casting himself in the role of a warrior, inevitably created enemies for Julius - many of whom accused him of sodomy. Accounts are in agreement, nevertheless, that contemporaries thought Julius II to be a sodomite. The Venetian diarist Giralomo Priuli attested: "He brought along with him his catamites, that is to say, some very handsome young men with whom he was rumoured to have intercourse".

February 22, 1994: The ELCA defrocks Pastor Ross Merkel: (see Feb 19)

March 7: Feast day of SS. Perpetua and Felicity, martyrs (According to all calendars)- The popularity of the story of Saints Perpetua and Felicitas was largely due to the appeal of love between two women. Five Christians were martyred together at Carthage on March 7, 203, suffering death at the hands of wild animals and the sword, but only Perpetua and Felicitas captured the fancy of the Christian community, apparently because of the tale of the two women comforting each other in jail, suffering martyrdom together as friends, and bestowing upon each other the kiss of peace as they met their end, charmed the tastes of the age.

March 10: Feast day of St. Anastasia/Anastasios the Patrician (or "of Constantinople") (According to the Orthodox and Old Roman Calendar – also celebrated on August 28th). Anastasia/Anastasios was a female born ascetic who wore male monastic habits. Anastasia fled the advances of the emperor Justinian by hiding in the Egyptian desert as the monk Anastasios or St. Matrona of Perge. Zir birth sex was uncovered when Anastasios' earlobes were found to be pierced.

March 15: Feast day of St. Longinus the Centurion (According to the Old Roman Calendar also celebrated on Oct 16 in the Orthodox Calendar). St. Longinus is known as being the Centurion that pierced Jesus' side and the Centurion who notes "surly this is man is the Son of God." Some scholars have also wondered if this is the same centurion that Jesus meets in the Gospel of Luke (chapter 7) and cures his slave/boy.

As Fr. Johh O'Neil has pointed out, there are several aspects to this story which might lend it to a queer reading. In the first place it seems somewhat odd that a centurion would be so caring about a slave, caring enough to risk ridicule by approaching a Jewish miracle worker for help. The underlying Greek text intensifies this suspicion of a possible same-sex relationship. Tom Horner, author of David Loved Jonathan: Homosexuality in Biblical Times, points out that in Matthew, the earlier account and directed to a Greek-speaking Jewish audience, the word for servant is "pais" - which means "boy", but can also mean "servant", and, given the rather greater than average concern for a servant demonstrated by the centurion, can also mean "lover". Luke (7:1), who was writing in a much more Greek milieu changes the word "pais" to the much more neutral "doulos" ("servant" or "slave"), presumably aware of its homosexual implications to any reader with a Greek cultural background. Jesus, clearly, does not condemn the centurion in this story of faith.

March 18: Anniversary of the day that Catalina de Erauso/Francisco Loyola escaped from the nunnery and began living as a man (March 18, 1600)- 1592-?1650; Dona Catalina de Erauso, nicknamed "the Lieutenant nun," ran away to Latin America at age 15 to become a soldier and took the name Francisco Loyola. He (gendered pronoun used in Erauso/Loyola's autobiography) became engaged to at least two women but vanished before the weddings. After being condemned to death several times he begged for the church's pardon and entered a convent in Peru (after revealing his anatomy of birth). Pope Urban VIII issued her a papal license to dress in masculine attire.

98

March 20, 2002: Censure of Holy Trinity Lutheran Church in Key West, Florida: (see September 22)

March 23, 2001: Censure of Abiding Peace: (see October 28)

March 26, 2006: Installation of Pastor Robert "Bob" Goldstein at St. Francis Lutheran in San Francisco- Pastor Bob is a member of the Extraordinary Lutheran Ministries roster, who before coming to St. Francis, served congregations in New Jersey and Chicago for the past 30 years. Born in Melbourne, Australia. He received his B.A. in Biblical Languages and Literature from Abilene Christian University in 1965, and a B.D. and S.T.M. at Yale, where he specialized in the philosophical writings of Wittgenstein and Kierkegaard under Professor Paul Holmer. He received a Ph.D. from Princeton Theological Seminary in 1982 in Philosophical Theology.

March 27: Death of King James I of England (and VI of Scotland)- 1566-1625; King James I is not the first queer English ruler (Henry III, Elizabeth I), but he is the one that has the most profound influence on the Christian Church. King James I, who likened himself and his beloved George Villiers to the relationship between Jesus and Saint John the Evangelist, commissioned the King James Version (KJV) of the Bible. The KJV is the first bible to translate biblical passages in a way condemns homosexual relationships in an attempt to criticize the king without the risk of beheading.

Easter: The Miraculous Sex Change of the Abbot of Drimnagh- After preparing for the Easter feast The Abbot of Drimnagh (near Dublin) fell asleep and awoke to discover that zir sword had been replaced with a spindle, zir tunic was replaced with a woman's dress and zir beard miraculously disappeared. Soon after, the abbot encounters a handsome young man who works at the Crumlin church, they fall instantly in love and marry. They live together for seven years and have seven children. On the way to the church in Drimnagh for the Easter vigil, the abbot becomes nervous that zir former wife will recognize zir, so the abbot falls asleep in the same spot and is transformed back into a man. The courts decide to grant four of the children to the handsome young man and three to the abbot and they remain friends to the end of their days.

April 11, 2004: Installation of Pastor Jenny Mason at Central City Lutheran Mission (see January)

April 20: Feast Day of St. Hildegonde of Neuss nr. Cologne (According to the Old Roman Calendar)- A nun who lived under the name "Brother Joseph" in the Cistercian monastery of Schoenau near Heidelberg.

April 20: Feast Day of St. Anselm of Canterbury, bishop & doctor (According to all Western Calendars)- (1033?-1109); In the late Middle Ages the attempt to use philosophy to explain Christian faith was called scholasticism. The founder of scholasticism was St. Anselm, a man who combined the careers of philosopher, theologian, monk, and archbishop. Anselm was born at Aosta, Italy, in about 1033. In 1057 he entered the Benedictine monastery at Bec, in northwestern France. In 1078 he became the abbot there. As Anselm's abilities and great learning became known, Bec became one of the leading schools of philosophy and theology. While on inspection tours of monasteries in England, Anselm had been befriended by King William I. In 1093 William I's son and successor, William II Rufus, appointed Anselm archbishop of Canterbury. His term of office was an unhappy one, for he immediately became involved in one of the major conflicts of the time--the investiture controversy. At issue was whether a king had the right to invest a bishop with the symbols of his office. On this issue Anselm resisted both William II and his successor, Henry I. The matter was finally resolved in Anselm's favor by the Westminster Agreement of 1107. He lived only two more years, dying on April 21, 1109.

While the sexual practices of Anselm are unknown, he had emotional relationships with Lanfranc and then a succession of his own pupils. He would address his letters to his "beloved lover" [dilecto dilitori]: ""Wherever you go my love follows you, and wherever I remain my desire embraces you...How then could I forget you? He who is imprisoned on my heart like a seal on wax-how could he be removed from my memory? Without saying a word I know that you love [amor] me, and without my saying a word, you know that I love you." Anselm was also one of the first saints to refer to Jesus as mother.[201]

April 23: Feast Day of St. George (According to all calendars)- St. George is, along with St. Nicholas, without any question among the most popular of all saints in history. The odd thing is that nothing whatsoever can be established about him as a historical figure. George at one stage is about to marry, but is prevented by Christ. As the text said "[George] did not know that Christ was keeping him as a pure virginal bridegroom for himself". Later on after mind-boggling escapades [George is killed and resurrected a number or times in his myths], Christ welcomes George into Heaven with bridal imagery. In these texts, George is presented as the bridegroom of Christ. Bridal imagery is quite common in discourse about Christ, but usually male saints are made into "brides of Christ," but with George a same sex marital imagery is used. Ironically, St. George is the patron saint of scouting (among other things)!

April 24: Death of Rev. Phil Knutson- Phil Knutson ended his struggle with AIDS on April 24, 1994, was an ordained Lutheran pastor who served as assistant director for campus ministry at the ELCA headquarters in Chicago from 1988-1994. For ten years, he also served as advisor to the Lutheran Student Movement. It has been said that "he killed himself out of the shame placed upon him by the Church for being gay and having AIDS." His stole is on display with the "For All Saints" Stoles Project of the Lutheran Network for Inclusive Vision.

---

[201] See Bynum, Jesus as Mother.

April 26, 1992: Ordination of Pastor Jane Ralph: Pastor Jane Ralph, a member of the Extraordinary Lutheran Ministries roster, was ordained April 24th 1992 and served as pastor of St. James Lutheran Church, Director of The Child Abuse Prevention Ministry in a synodical call to Metropolitan Lutheran Ministry and as pastor of King of Glory Lutheran Church all in or around Kansas City, MO before being removed from the ELCA roster in 1998.

Since then Jane's ministry has taken many turns and she has found herself working in media advocacy for GLAAD, homeless ministries and services at N Street Village in DC and COTS in Burlington, VT, and as Multicultural Outreach Coordinator for Holden Village. Along the way her unpaid work included significant investment in Soulforce, Anti-racism work, faith based community organizing and leadership in LLGM.

In June 2007 Jane was selected as Executive Director of the Clarina Howard Nichols Center in Morrisville, VT a feminist organization dedicated to ending sexual and domestic violence through survivor centered service and advocacy.

April 26, 2000: Censure of University Lutheran Chapel: (see November 7)

April 28, 2001: Ordination of Pastor Anita Hill: Pastor Anita is a member of the Extraordinary Lutheran Ministry roster and was ordained on April 28, 2001. She has been on staff at St. Paul-Reformation since 1994. In addition, she served as Ministry Associate of Wingspan Ministry of the congregation from 1982-90. Some of her other professional experience includes five years as a diversity trainer for Family Service of St. Paul and as an AIDS ministry advocate for two years at Lutheran Social Services of Minnesota. Anita has served on the ELCA Task Force on Human Sexuality and as a member of the Saint Paul Area Synod Board for Church and Society. Anita has an M.A. degree in Religious Studies and M. Div. Degree from United Theological Seminary of the Twin Cities.

April 29, 2001: Installation of Pastor Anita Hill at St. Paul – Reformation (see April 28)

April 29: Feast day of Saint Catherine of Siena (According to the Old Roman Calendar; patron saint of fire prevention)- 1347-1380 CE; Chaterine was an Italian Catholic nun that began having visions at age six. Catherine's spiritual advisor Saint Raymund of Capua had a vision of Catherine's face transformed into a bearded man, symbolizing her mystical union with Chirst by becoming spiritually transgender.

May 2, 2004: Installation of Pastor Dan Hooper at Hollywood Lutheran Church: Pastor Dan Hooper, member of the Extraordinary Lutheran Ministries roster, was ordained in the former American Lutheran Church in 1974. He served as a Lutheran pastor in Arizona and Southern California until he was "outed" and removed from the ELCA's clergy roster in 1988.

May 8: Feast day of Julian of Norwich, mystic (According to the Church of England and Episcopal Book of Common Prayer)- Sporting a male name, Mother Julian was one of the foremost English mystics of the middle ages. As a young woman she had series of intense visions, or "showings" as she said, of Jesus. She then lived as an anchoress, a sort of local hermit, for the rest of her life meditating and writing down the meditations on these visions. Julian, although no feminist, experienced God(dess) directly as "our mother", and experienced God as pure love. She also saw Jesus as a loving mother, full of warm and care for her children. Julian's immensely attractive spirituality emphasize that God love's human beings, and that in the end "all will be well, and all shall be well, and all will be well."

May 10: Birthday of Pastor Cindy Crane: Pastor Cindy Crane is a former member of the Extraordinary Lutheran Ministries Roster who was ordained in 1988. She served ELCA parishes for 10 years mainly in western Wisconsin and also in Minneapolis.

May 12, 2002: Ordination of Pastor Sharon Stalkfleet: Pastor Sharon is a member of the Extraordinary Lutheran Ministries roster who was ordained extraordinarily on May 12, 2002 at St. Paul Lutheran Church in Oakland, Calif. She was initially called by four congregations: Resurrection, St. Paul and Trinity Lutheran Churches (Oakland) and Trinity Lutheran Church (Alameda). Immanuel Lutheran Church (Alameda) issued Sharron a call in January of 2003. Bethlehem Lutheran (Oakland) and Lutheran Church of the Cross (Berkeley) also support this ministry to serve as a chaplain to nursing homes in the Bay Area.

May 14: Death of Pope John XII- 938-964; Taking office at the age of 18 after his father, Pope John XII was a bisexual drawn to paganism, He was elected to the office because of his father's powerful connections. Accused of turning a sacred place into "a whorehouse," gambling, killing, toasting the devil and taking money to declare people Bishops (one of whom was ten years old), church authorities deposed him after finding him hiding in the woods, and replaced him with Pope Leo VIII.

May 16, 2008: Ordination of Pastor Lionel Ketola in Newmarket Ontario: Pastor Ketola, member of the Extraordinary Lutheran Ministries roster, was called to Holy Cross where he served briefly as associate pastor and Ambassador of Reconciliation. Ketola became the first legally married gay man to be ordained in the Lutheran church. Later, the congregation and the pastors who participated in the ordination were censured by the local bishop, who is investigating whether or not to further discipline the congregation.

Lionel began his candidacy process with the Evangelical Lutheran Church in Canada (ELCIC) in 1985. After coming out to his bishop in 1986 Lionel's internship site was cancelled and he faced the prospect of being dropped from the master of divinity program at the Lutheran Theological Seminary at Saskatoon. While Lionel was eventually allowed to finish his degree, his progress towards approval for ordination was halted.

May 20: Feast Day of St. Alcuin of Tuirs (According to the Episcopal Book of Common Prayer) - (c. 735- 804); Alcuin was a leading figure in the Carolingian renaissance of the late 7th and early 8th centuries. The prominence of love in Alcuin's writings, all of which are addressed to other males, is strikingly passionate. He wrote to a friend: "I think of your love and friendship with such sweet memories, reverend bishop, that I long for that lovely time when I may be able to clutch the neck of your sweetness with the fingers of my desires. Alas, if only it were granted to me, as it was to Habakkuk [Dan. 14:32-38], to be transported to you, how I would sink into your embraces,...how much would I cover, with tightly pressed lips, not only your eyes, ears and mouth, but also your every finger and toe, not once but many a time."

May 26, 1968: Ordination of Pastor Donn Rosenauer: Pastor Donn Rosenauer is a member of the Extraordinary Lutheran Ministries roster who has served Lutheran congregations in Watford City, ND, Rochester, MN; Zumbrota, MN; Lincoln, NE and Seattle, WA. During his seven years at Zumbrota, congregational giving increased 80 percent. In Zumbrota he spearheaded a drive that resulted in building a chapel for the community hospital. In Seattle he chaired a successful fund raising drive for the Northwest Religious Broadcasting Commission. As a Paul Harris fellow, Donn raised significant dollars for the Rotary Foundation.

May 26, 1985: Ordination of Pastor Cindy Witt - Pastor Cindy Witt was initially excluded from ministry for being a women until she was ordained in the ALC in 1985. Cindy has a stole on display with the "For All Saints" Stoles Project of the Lutheran Network for Inclusive Vision. Witt is roster by Extraordinary Lutheran Ministries.

Pentecost or May 29, 1966: Ordination of Pastor Paul Brenner at Zion Evangelical Lutheran Church in Owensville, Montana

(LCMS): Paul is a member of the Extraordinary Lutheran Ministries roster who began attending St. Francis Lutheran Church, San Francisco, CA, in 2002 and was taken into membership at the Easter Vigil, 2003. He has served on the Worship Committee, the Board of the Friends of St. Francis Childcare Center, the St. Vincent de Paul Committee, facilitated the Adult Study Group for over two years, served as an interim pastor for a year and a half during St. Francis' vacancy, and sings in the choir. A motet he composed was sung by the Men and Boys choir of St. Thomas Lutheran Church, Leipzig, Germany. He has 30 years of leadership in the hospice movement, serving programs in Jacksonville, Florida, West Palm Beach, Florida, Rockville, Md. and Jacob Perlow Hospice at Beth Israel Medical Center, New York City. He served ten years as pastor of a Lutheran inner city parish in Jacksonville, Florida, and also served as an interim pastor in that community. Presently he volunteers in the Creative Healing Project, a program with his son, Matthew, which provides art experiences for children and teens diagnosed with potentially life threatening medical conditions.

May 30: Feast day of St. Joan of Arc (According to the Old Roman Calendar)- c.1412-1431; Joan, who was executed at the age of 19, is the national heroine of France. Zie also refused to wear women's clothes and had zir hair cut in the typical male "basin" style of the day. Even during her trial zie insisted on male attire, an insistence which angered her prosecutors. Charles VII had made no effort to save Joan. Some 25 years later he did aid her family to appeal the case to the pope, and in 1456 a papal court annulled the judgment of 1431. On May 16, 1920, Joan of Arc was canonized a saint by the Roman Catholic church.

May 30, 1992: Ordination of Pastor Cindy Coleman: Pastor Cindy is member of the Extraordinary Lutheran Ministries roster.

June 1967: Ordination date of a pastor in the ELCA- Ordained into the American Lutheran Church, this unknown pastor writes: "Now questions are being asked, people are being removed from the

ELCA, and others are being prevented from following God's call along the path to ordination. After 32 years of faithful ministry to this church, I am not about to start answering questions that should never be asked in the first place. " This pastor has a stole on display with the "For All Saints" Stoles Project of the Lutheran Network for Inclusive Vision and is signed by others who supported his stance.

June 1972: Ordination of Pastor Nate Gruel: Pastor Nate is rostered by Extraordinary Lutheran Ministries. Ordained a pastor within the Missouri Synod of the Lutheran church in 1972, Pastor Nate served two parishes in Indiana over a period of seven years. Since then, he has been employed as a graphic artist in the newspaper industry. He and his partner of 17 years, Paul Monaghan, moved to Florida in 2003.

June 3: Feast day of Saint Paula of Avila, martyr and virgin (according to the Old Roman Calendar) : Was granted a beard and possibly a total sex change when zie asked Christ to protect her from a man who was interested in zir sexually. According to custom, Paula was a virgin in Nicomedia who was moved to give assistance and care to St. Lucillian. Paula was arrested for aiding Lucillian and four Christian youths and was tortured and sent to Constantinople, where zie was beheaded.

June 3, 1984: Ordination of Rev. Joanne Williamsen- Rev. Joanne Williamsen was asked to resign from Luther seminary in 1978. She was ordained UCC.

June 4, 1965: Ordination of Pastor David Abernethy-Deppe: Pastor David is a former member of the Extraordinary Lutheran Ministries roster who currently serves as a priest in the Episcopal church.

June 4, 1978: Ordination of Pastor Lyle Beckman: Pastor Lyle Beckman a member of both the ELCA the Extraordinary Lutheran

Ministries roster, currently service under call of the Sierra Pacific Synod as the Night Minister in San Francisco.

June 4, 1972: Ordination of Pastor Paul A. Johnson- Ordained at his home church in Ladysmith, Wisconsin, Paul served three Wisconsin parishes between 1972 and 1988. In June of 1988 Paul was installed as assistant to the Bishop of the La Crosse Area Synod, ELCA. Paul resigned at the request of Bishop Stefan Guttormsson on May 22,1991 as an alternative to a disciplinary hearing. The Bishop then publicly outed Paul by issuing a press release the following day which appeared with a picture in the La Crosse Tribune announcing: "Gay Pastor Resigns Post" on May 24th. Paul went on to become a member of the Lesbian and Gay Persons Ministry Team of the Southeastern Iowa Synod. Paul has a stole on display with the "For All Saints" Stoles Project of the Lutheran Network for Inclusive Vision.

June 7, 1986: Ordination of Pastor Jeffery Nelson: Former member of the Extraordinary Lutheran Ministries roster.

June 8: Ordination of Pastor Ross Merkel: (see Feb. 19)

June 9: Feast day of St. Pelagia/Pelagios (According to the Old Roman Calendar; also celebrated on Oct 8 according to the Orthodox Calendar)- Pelagia/Pelagios was a female born ascetic who wore male monastic habits. Pelagia/Pelagios was an actress, a notoriously evil and despised profession in the early days of the church. Zie acted in Antioch under the name of Margaret until Pelagia/Pelagios came to repent of evil ways by the preaching of St. Nonnus. Since at that time it was impossible to allow a member of the acting profession to be baptised until the very point of death, zie was only permitted, after many dramatic protestations of sincerity, to be put under the care of the deaconess Romana whose duties consisted of taking care of catechumens. Pelagia/Pelagios gave away all her finery and treasures and was ultimately baptized, confirmed and was allowed to receive communion. Zie then slipped away from Antioch dressed as a monk and went to Jerusalem where

Pelagia/Pelagios built a hermitage on the Mount of Olives where zie lived for three years until zir death. Known as a monk and a eunuch, when Pelagia/Pelagios was discovered at zir death to have the body of a "female" the mourners chanted "Glory be to thee, Lord Jesus, for thou hast many hidden treasures on earth, female as well as male.

June 10, 1979: Ordination of Pastor Steve Robertson: Pastor Steve is a member of the Extraordinary Lutheran Ministries roster and a graduate of Luther Seminary. Steve served as Associate Pastor of Our Saviour's Lutheran Church, East Bethel, Minnesota before becoming the Senior Pastor of Cambridge Lutheran Church, Cambridge, MN. Following an 11 year ministry in Cambridge, Steve was called to become the senior pastor of Atonement Lutheran Church in Overland Park, KS. His last call in the ELCA was as the senior pastor of Gustavus Adolphus Lutheran Church, St. Paul, MN. In 2006 Steve was removed from ELCA roster after a three year leave of absence and discernment process. Following this period in his life Steve fully came out as a gay man in a same sex committed relationship. Steve is currently serving as a Spiritual Coordinator/Bereavement Counselor for AseraCare Hospice, Bloomington. Steve and his partner, Jeff Coffman, live in a suburb of St Paul (Little Canada) and are currently members of St Paul Reformation Lutheran Church.

June 12, 2001: Censure of St. Paul – Reformation (see April 28)

June 13, 1971: Ordination of Pastor Michael Hiller: Pastor Michael is a former member of the Extraordinary Lutheran Ministries roster who served at St. Francis Lutheran in San Francisco and who is currently a priest in the Episcopal church.

June 16, 1974: Ordination of Pastor Jonathon Abernethy-Deppe: Pastor Jonathon is a former member of the Extraordinary Lutheran Ministries roster who currently serves as a priest in the Episcopal church.

June 16, 2007: Ordination of Pastor Dawn Roginski at St. Francis Lutheran in San Francisco, CA: Pastor Dawn Roginski is a member of the Extraordinary Lutheran Ministries roster who grew up Catholic in Minneapolis, Minnesota. She earned an undergraduate psychology degree from the University of Minnesota and began a career in counseling. Dawn then earned an M.A. in Counseling Psychology from St. Mary's University of Minnesota. Despite obstacles due to her sexual orientation, Dawn received her Master of Divinity degree at Luther Seminary December in 2002, completing her internship at Lord of Light Lutheran Campus Ministry in Ann Arbor, MI.

In 2003, Dawn became a part-time chaplain and part-time youth care worker at a residential treatment center for children in Kansas City, MO, providing care for seriously emotionally disturbed children and youth. Dawn developed a youth ministry program from the ground up, including groups and worship. As her programs grew, she was offered the position of full-time chaplain. Dawn is currently a pastor at St. Francis Lutheran in San Francisco.

June 20, 1992: Ordination of Pastor Terry Hagensen at Zion Lutheran Church in Camas, Washington: Pastor Terry is a member of the Extraordinary Lutheran Ministries roster, and a graduate of Wartburg Theological Seminary in Dubuque, Iowa.

June 22: Feast Day of St. Paulinus of Nola, bishop (According to both the New and Old Roman Calendars)- 353-431; Paulinus of Nola was an important figure in the Christian Roman Empire. Although he was married, he was also passionately in love with his fellow Christian and teacher, the writer Ausonius. Later in life Paulinus distanced himself from Ausonius, a victim perhaps of a narrowing view of sexual ethics.

June 27, 1976: Ordination of Pastor Jim Bischoff in the American Lutheran Church (ALC): Pastor Jim is a member of the Extraordinary Lutheran Ministries roster who was dismissed from ministry after 23 years of ordained ministry in the ALC and the

ELCA, who noted that: "I feel that I am a better pastor now that I am 'out' than I ever was before. The Holy Spirit has given me a sense of freedom and liberation to truly be the pastor that God has called me to be."

Jim has a blue stole is on display with the "For All Saints" Stoles Project of the Lutheran Network for Inclusive Vision, because "both Advent and the color blue are very much centered on hope. Hope is what I have for the ELCA. Hope that the Spirit of God will be at work and bring an end to the policy that discriminates and is harmful to both clergy (including prospective clergy) and congregations."

June 27, 1993: Ordination of Pastor Edward "Ned" O'Donnell: Pastor Ned is a member of the Extraordinary Lutheran Ministries roster.

June 29: Feast day of St. Paul (According to the New Roman Calendar)- d.67; At first glance, the argument that St. Paul was gay seems absurd, however as Anglican Bishop of Newark John Spong has pointed out there is also evidence that leads one to suspect Paul might have been queer in some way. The fact he was never married, unusual for a Jew of his time, his companionship with a series of younger men, especially St. Timothy, his mention of an unnamed "thorn in the flesh" and, possibly, his disdain for some types of exploitative homoeroticism in his period, all raise questions, questions which cannot be answered it must be admitted, about his sexuality. It should also be added that despite Paul's modern reputation for placing women lower than men, he also penned revolutionary words about the absolute equality of all believers in Christ, a complete destruction of prevailing social codes and norms that has only intermittently played out in full in Church history.

June 30, 1985: Ordination of Pastor Steve Sabin: Pastor Steve, former member of the Extraordinary Lutheran Ministries roster, was ordained to Word and Sacrament ministry by the Lutheran Church in America in June 1985. Before coming to Christ Church Luther in San Francisco in April 2001, Pastor Steve was the Pastor of Lord of Life Lutheran Church in Ames, Iowa for 16 years. In addition to his parish responsibilities, Pastor Steve has served as a national leader in ecumenical relations and has extensive experience in social advocacy and community development.

Pastor Steve graduated from the Lutheran School of Theology at Chicago with a Master of Divinity degree. He holds a Bachelor of Science degree in Psychology with a minor in Classics from the University of Iowa. Pastor Steve took his chaplaincy training at Rush-Presbyterian-St. Luke's Hospital and Medical School in Chicago, and did an internship at Emmanuel Lutheran Church in Manchester, Connecticut.

July 14, 1991: Ordination of Pastor Roy "Dale" Poland: Pastor Dale is a member of the Extraordinary Lutheran Ministries roster who works as a hospice chaplain Dale was ordained and installed as Associate Pastor of St. Mark Evangelical Lutheran Church on July 14, 1991. A native of Rio, West Virginia, Dale graduated from Gettysburg Lutheran Theological Seminary with academic honors in New Testament Studies on May 17, 1991. Previously, he had earned a Bachelors' of Science Degree in Forestry and Wildlife Resources from Virginia Polytechnic Institute and State University in 1987.

July 17: Feast day of St. Marina/os of Antioch (According to the Orthodox Calendar; also celebrated on July 20 on the Old Roman Calendar as St. Margaret)- Mariana/os of Antioch was a female born ascetic who wore male monastic habits.

July 20: Feast day of St. Wilgefortis (According to the Old Roman Calendar)- This bearded woman saint is said to have prayed to God in order to disfigure her body so that she would not have to go through with an estranged marriage. Her father tried to force her to get married by having her wear a long veil to the wedding ceremony. However, her suitor refused to marry Wilgefortis when the veil was lifted. She was crucified by her father the King of Portugal because of her "unaturalness."

July 20: Feast day of St. Marina/Marinos of Sicily (According to the Orthodox Calendar)- Mariana/os of Sicily was a female born ascetic who wore male monastic habits.

July 21: Feast Day of St. Daniel, the prophet (According to the Old Roman Calendar; listed at Dec. 17/18 in the Orthodox Calendars)- c.650BCE; Known to have worn a coat of many colors that may have signified admittance into a queer cult, the prophet Daniel was understood by Byzantine commentators, including St. John Chrysostom, to have been taken to serve as a eunuch, the major defined sexual minority of the ancient world, at the King of Babylon's court. Note the emphasis on the physical beauty of the four young men. He is, nevertheless, along with David one of the heroes of the Jewish Scriptures. Fr. Helminiak reports suggestions that "eunuch" was just a general way of referring to "homosexuals" in the period, although remains merely a suggestion. More interesting has been discussion of the "favor and tender love" Daniel enjoyed with the chief eunuch.

July 21: SS. Symeon of Emesa and John (According to Orthodox Calendars)- Symeon the the "Holy Fool" of Emesa supposedly lived in the sixth century. The story itself is about a same-sex relationship. Symeon, with his mother, and John, with his new wife, meet on a pilgrimage to Jerusalem. They become friends and "would no longer part from each other". In fact they abandon their families and go together to dedicate their lives to God. In the monastery they first join, they are tonsured by the abbot who blesses them together. This seems to refer to some early monastic version of the adelphopoiia ceremony. As with St. George (April 23), both Symeon and John are referred to as the "pure bridegrooms (nymphoi) of Christ."

The two men then leave the monastery and live together as hermits for twenty-nine years. There is no suggestion that they had a sexual relationship, but that they were very much a same sex couple. When the extent of the relationship is revealed, Symeon decides to leave. John says to Symeon "..Please, for the Lord's sake, do not leave wretched me....Rather for the sake of Him who joined us, do not wish to be parted from your brother. You know that, after God, I have no one except you, my brother, but I renounced all and was bound to you, and now you wish to leave me in the desert, as in an open sea. Remember that day when we drew lost and went down to the Lord Nikon, that we agreed not to be separated from one another. Remember that fearful day when we were clothed in the holy habit, and we two were as one soul, so that all were astonished at our love. Don't forget the words of the great monk...Please don't lest I die and God demands an account of my soul from You."

These words fail to move Symeon, who insists on going. He urges John to pray with him. After which this scene occurs: "After they had prayed for many hours and had kissed each other on the breast and drenched them with their tears, John let go of Symeon and traveled together with him a long distance, for his soul would not let him be separated from him. But whenever Symeon said to him 'Turn Back, Brother', he heard the word as if a knife separated him from his body, and again he asked if he could accompany him a little further. Therefore, when Symeon forced him, he turned back to his cell drenching the earth with tears."

July 22: Feast day of Saint Catherine of Genoa (According to the Old Roman Calendar) 1477-1510 CE; Catherine was a noble woman who married at sixteen, devoted herself to helping the poor and it was reported that in 1493 she kissed a nun of the third order or tertiary as a sign of piety and healing.

July 24: Feast day of Saint Boris, prince and martyr (dia natalis; patron saint of Moscow and Princes)-985-1015 CE; Boris was a prince from Kiev, who had a squire named George that he loved beyond reasoning. George flung his body on top of Boris' when he was about to be assassinated.

July 25, 2004: Ordination of Pastor Jay Wiesner at Bethany Lutheran in Minneapolis, Minnesota: Pastor Jay is a member of the Extraordinary Lutheran Ministries roster who graduated from Concordia College in Moorhead, Minnesota with a BA in religion. After college, he attended Wartburg Theological Seminary in Dubuque, Iowa. During his senior year, he publicly came out to the faculty and students at Wartburg and left to take some time off. He finished his Master of Divinity degree in 2002 and immediately began work at Bethany Lutheran Church in Minneapolis, Minnesota, as Pastoral Minister of Outreach. He was called and ordained by Bethany on July 25, 2004 where he served from 2002-2008.

Jay currently serves as pastor of University Lutheran Church of the Incarnation, an ELCA congregation in Philadelphia, Pennsylvania and is also pastoral director of The Naming Project.

The Naming Project is a faith-based youth group serving youth of all sexual and gender identities. The primary focus is to provide a place for youth who are gay, lesbian, bisexual, transgender, queer or questioning to learn, grow, and share their experiences. In this way The Naming Project is a space in which youth can comfortably discuss faith and who they understand themselves to be--whether gay, lesbian, bisexual, transgender or straight.

July 26: Birthday of Pastor Cindy Witt: Pastor Cindy is a former member of the Extraordinary Lutheran Ministries roster.

July 26: Death of Pope Paul II-1417-1471; Known for his "effeminate behavior, vanity, beauty, and extravagant clothing," Pope Paul II is said to have died in the throws of homoerotic passions from a heart attack. After Paul II's death, one of his successors suggested that he should be called Maria Pietissima, "Our Lady of Pity", because he was inclined to break into tears at times of crisis . However, some commentators have suggested that the nickname was due to Paul II's propensity to enjoy dressing up in sumptuous ecclesiastical finery.

July 26, 2008: Ordination of Pastor Lura Groen in Houston, Texas: Pastor Lura, member of the Extraordinary Lutheran Ministries roster, was called to Grace Evangelical Lutheran Church. Pastor Lura attended St. John's College in Annapolis MD, studying the Great Books Program. Prior to seminary, Pastor Lura was a two-year member of Lutheran Volunteer Corps, serving as a case manager to homeless people in Baltimore MD and Washington

DC. Lura continued her social service work as an employment coach before attending seminary at the Lutheran Theological Seminary at Philadelphia.

Pastor Lura finds God by embracing community life. While attending LTSP, Lura formed and led an LGBTQ support group on campus, served on Community Council, participated in the Inter-Racial Dialogue Group, was a Member of the School of the Americas Planning Committee, (to educate the seminary about our country's foreign policy towards Latin America, and attend the protest in Ft. Benning Georgia), and published numerous reflections in the student newspaper. During the 2004-2005 Academic year, she served as Student Body President, presiding over the merger of two student bodies into one. Her awards included the Winters Scholarship for academic excellence and potential for ministry, the Traci L. Maul Award for leadership potential for ministry, active contribution to seminary life, and academic strength. Atonement-Asbury Park Preaching Award, and the Deans List.

July 31, 2001: Bishop Paul W. Egertson left his office one month early honoring a promise he made that he would resign if he violated church rules pertaining to gay and lesbian church members. Bishop Egertson's resignation took place after he participated with three retired bishops and 150 ELCA clergy in the ordination service for Anita Carol Hill in St. Paul, Minnesota, on April 28.

August 1, 2004: Installation of Pastor Jay Wiesner at Bethany Lutheran Church: (see July 25)

August 6, 1989: Ordination of Pastor Douglas Mose- Douglas was forced to resign on Easter Sunday, 1994 and was removed from the ELCA clergy roster on June 1, 1997. Doug was a student leader at the University of Minnesota, St Paul campus ministry and has been the director of the Voices of Faith for Equality Colorado. Doug has a stole on display with the "For All Saints" Stoles Project of the

Lutheran Network for Inclusive Vision and is signed by others who supported his stance.

August 11: Feast day of Cardinal John Henry Newman (dia natalis)-1801-90; John Henry Newman, the most prominent 19th century-convert to Roman Catholicism, is best known for his writings, especially his superb spiritual biography, Apologia Pro Vita Sua. It is certain that Newman was sexually abstinent throughout his life, nevertheless he spent most of his life with his closest friend, Fr. Ambrose St. John. Some reports state that he lay all night on Ambrose St. John's bed after Ambrose's death, and, stipulated in his will that he wished to be, and was in fact, buried in the same grave as Fr. St. John at Rednal in the English midlands.

August 12: Death of Pope Sixtus IV- 1414-1484; Born Francesco della Rovere, Pope Sixtus IV apointed his nephew and beloved, Raphael Riaro, to the offices of Papal Chamberlain and Bishop of Ostia. Pope Sixtus IV is also known for founding the Sistine Chapel.

August 13, 1988: Ordination Pastor Deb Click: Pastor Deb is a former member of the Extraordinary Lutheran Ministries roster.

August 14, 1978: The Lutheran Student Movement rebukes the church for silence- a 300 student assembly held at Wittenburg University in Springfeild, Ohio adopted a 1,400 word paper with little debate, no criticisms and only 2 schools' dissents. The future leaders of the church declared: "This means that regardless of.. theological positions on... homosexuality, we believe the priestly imperative is to be present with to bring grace to, be supportive of, love and refrain from judging people of any group." Efforts to prepare this statement date back to 1972.

August 18: Death of Pope Alexander VI- 1431-1503; Pope Alexander VI, born Roderic Borja, was allegedly bisexual. Fathering several children with several mistresses, he was also thought to have had several handsome male pages as lovers as well as a man named Jem.

August 19: St. Sussanah/John- Female born ascetic who wore male monastic habits. Refused to give up her identity even when accused and condemned falsely for seduction and rape.

August 20: Feast day of St. Bernard of Clairvaux (According to the Old Roman Calendar)- 1090-1153 CE; Bernard was a French Christian churchman who was a merciless zealot, had an erotic relation with Jesus, his divine lover and husband. After Bernard's death, many French individuals believed that if they passed under the rainbow of St. Bernard that they would undergo a gender metamorphosis.

August 26, 1974: Ordination of Pastor Dan Hooper: (see May 2)

August 28: Feast of St. Augustine of Hippo, bishop & doctor (According to all Western Calendars)- 354-430; The bishop of Hippo in Roman Africa for 35 years, St. Augustine lived during the decline of Roman civilization on that continent. Considered the greatest of the Fathers of the Church in the West, he helped form Christian theology. Augustine has often been held responsible for the aggressive anti-sex stance of much of western Christian history, chiefly because of his linking the transmission of original sin with sexual activity. In fact, compared to some of the anti-sex zealots of his time, he was rather moderate in seeing at least some good in sex within marriage. At times he spoke violently against "sodomy", but as the extracts from his Confessions show, he was for a time completely in love with another man, whose death threw him into turmoil and brought him to faith. The most famous conversion in Christian history, after that of St. Paul, originated in one man's love for another.

August 28, 1978: Ordination of Pastor Pieter Oberholzer: Pastor Pieter Oberholzer is a member of the Extraordinary Lutheran

Ministries roster who serves as a Missionary in South Africa, and works with Inclusive and Affirming Ministries with lesbian, gay, bisexual and transgender people. Pieter is called by St. Francis Lutheran in San Francisco, CA.

September 1991: Ordination of Pastor Steve Rosebrock: Pastor Steve Rosebrock is a member of the Extraordinary Lutheran Ministries roster.

September 1: Feast day of St. Giles (patron saint of sterility among many other things)- 650-710; Known as a phallic saint whose penis was rubbed for fertility. More than vulgar representations of the phallus, phallic saints were benevolent symbols of prolificacy and reproductive fruitfulness, and objects of reverence and especial worship among barren women and young girls.

September 9: Birthday of Pastor Phyllis Zillhart: Phyllis was ordained on January 20, 1990 (see January) and served as the Associate Pastor for Outreach and Evangelism at St. Francis Lutheran Church, San Francisco.

In 1990, she founded Lutheran Lesbian and Gay Ministry along with his colleagues, Pastors Jeff Johnson and Ruth Frost, to provide an outreach to the lesbian, gay, bisexual and transgendered community of the San Francisco Bay Area. These three persons were the first openly lesbian and gay people to be ordained in the Lutheran Church.

September 11: Feast day of St. Theodora/Theodoros of Alexandria (According to the Orthodox Calendar)- Thodora/Theodoros was a female born ascetic who wore male monastic habits. Theodora, married a good man but was unfaithful to him. Zie was seized with remorse and fled disguised as a man. Theodora was admitted to a monastery under the name of Theodoric and lived there until zie was accused of having "fathered" a child. Expelled from the monastery, Theodora/Theodoros lived alone with the baby for seven years until zie was re-admitted to the monastery where Theodora/Theodoros lived a life of great humility until zir death.

September 11, 2004: Censure of Hollywood Lutheran Church: (see May 2)

September 14, 1991: Ordination of Pastor Dawn Marie Gregg: Pastor Dawn is a member of the Extraordinary Lutheran Ministries roster and a graduate of Pacific Lutheran Theological Seminary in Berkeley, California. Dawn has specialized in interim ministries in Oregon for over 10 years. She continues to live in   Eugene   and hopes to be active soon with a mission start in the Eugene area.

September 21: Feast day of St. Edward II, King of England (According to England)- 1284-1327; Edward II was king of England from 1307 to 1327. He was deposed in a rebellion led by his adulterous wife, and ultimately killed in Berkeley Castle. He was famous for his love of a number of men, most important Piers Gaveston, and later Hugh Dispenser. There is little doubt that Edward was, despite his marriage and children, predominantly gay. Despite the common knowledge of his sexuality, he was popularly regarded a saint and wonderworker for over two centuries. His successors fought to get him canonized in Rome. This official canonization was not forthcoming. This is not surprising since the politics of canonization meant that very few saints from the British Isles were canonized in the 14th and 15th centuries.

September 22, 2004: Censure of Bethany Lutheran Church, Minneapolis: (see July 25)

September 22, 1974: Ordination of Pastor Arlo David Peterson. Ordained as a Lutheran pastor in 1974, Arlo David Peterson served congregations on Long Island, New York, and in the New York City borough of Queens before moving to Key West in 1994 to become a case manager for AIDS Help, the local organization that has a multi-faceted response to the AIDS epidemic in the Florida

Keys. Arlo remained on the ELCA clergy roster until he was removed without his knowledge in 1999. He only became aware of his removal when the ELCA Board of Pensions contacted him two years later, inquiring about his status as he was still being covered by the ELCA pension and medical plans. It was only in April of 2001 that he received official word that he was off the ELCA clergy roster. Arlo is a member of the ELM Roster.

September 23: Feast Day of St. Theckla (Thekla) of Iconium (According to the Old Roman Calendar; also celebrated on Sept 24 in the Orthodox Calendar)- An enormously popular figure in early Christianity, zir acts chronicled in the Acts of Theckla and Paul were moved to the Apocrypha by St. Jerome. Theckla refuses to marry and begins to dress as a man while traveling with the Apostle Paul.

October 7: Feast day of SS. Sergius and Bacchus, martyrs (according to the Old Roman Calendar; Bacchus is recognized in the Arab calendar on October 1st)- d. circa. 297; Saints Sergius and Bacchus were two Roman soldiers and lovers. These saints were invoked repeatedly in the middle ages in the blessing of ceremonies of union for couples of the same sex. They were arrested and humiliated for being Christians. Bacchus was killed first, and then a few days later, Sergius. Their joint "passion" calls them "erastoi" - that is "erotic lovers", and after he died, Bacchus offers himself to Sergius as the prize for Sergius' martyrdom. The female clothes they were forced to wear may have been an early example of gay baiting (one thing that cannot be found among the saints is a male saint who voluntarily adopted women's clothes). Their cult was one of the most intense in the eastern Mediterranean, with a huge pilgrimage site at Sergiopolis (Rusapha).

October 8, 2001: Pastor Jenny Mason Asked to Resign from ELCA Roster (see January)

October 9: Feast day of St. Athanasia/Athanasios of Antioch (According to the Orthodox Calendar)- Athanasia/Athanasios was a female born ascetic who wore male monastic habits. Athanasia and zir husband Andronicus decided to live as ascetics after the death of their children. After staying twelve years in a convent, Athanasia/Athanasios went on a pilgrimage to Jerusalem on the advice of the abbot Daniel. On the way zie met Andronicus who did not recognize zir because of the disfigurement caused by zir harsh life. They traveled together and on their return Andronicus proposed they live together as fellow ascetics. "Athanasius" agreed on condition that they follow a strict rule of silence. This they did for twelve years until Athanasia/Athanasios' death, and Athanasia/Athanasios' true identity was not revealed to Andronicus until he was on the point of death himself.

October 21, 2006: Ordination of Pastor Erik Christensen at St Luke, Logan Square in Chicago: Pastor Erik is member of the Extraordinary Lutheran Church roster and a graduate of Candler School of Theology, Emory University (M.Div., '02) and the Lutheran Theological Seminary at Philadelphia (S.T.M., '04).

October 25, 2008: Ordination of Pastor Jodi Barry at in Minneapolis, Minnesota: Pastor Jody is the first pastor ordained and called by Extraordinary Lutheran Ministries to serve as a chaplain at Mercy Hospital. Barry is married to the Rev. Dr. Jenny Mason (see January) who is also a member of the Extraordinary Lutheran Ministries roster.

Jodi was baptized, raised, and confirmed at Gethsemane Lutheran Church in Maplewood, MN. She graduated from Bethel College, St. Paul, MN with a B.A. in Literature (1990). Jodi has felt called to ministry since high school. Jodi attended United Theological Seminary (UTS) of the Twin Cities, graduating in 2001 with a M.Div. A year of Clinical Pastoral Education (CPE) residency followed, 2001-2002.

October 28, 2000: Ordination of Pastor Donna Simon at Abiding Peace in Kansas City, Missouri: Pastor Donna is a member of the Extraordinary Lutheran Ministries Roster and a 1999 graduate of Pacific Lutheran Theological Seminary, Berkeley, CA.

October 29: Feast day of St. Anna/Euphemianos of Constantinople (According to the Orthodox Calendar)- Anna/Euphemianos was a female born ascetic who wore male monastic habits.

October 31, 1995: Pastor Rebecca J. Hostetler resigned from the ELCA roster - Called to intentional interim work where she worked with seven churches. Vision and Expectations was drafted while Rebecca was in seminary at Luther Seminary and the document was not a part of her certification process. Rebecca writes: "Initially, I went on leave from call moving back to St. Paul and enjoying the freedom of being 'out' within St. Paul-Reformation Lutheran Church. Eventually, I resigned from the clergy roster knowing that I could not subscribe to the policy that came with the full document of Vision and Expectations and is accepted by the church at large."

Rebecca's red stole was presented to Pastor Anita Hill at her ordination and has subsequently been presented to each Extraordinary Lutheran Ministries roster member who has been ordained since Anita's ordination: Pastors Sharon Stalkfleet (May 12), Craig Minich (February 18), Jay Weisner (July 25), Erik Christensen (October 21), Megan Rohrer (November 18), Dawn Roginski, Jen Rude (November 17), Jen Nagel (January 19), Lionel Ketola (May 16), Jodi Barry (October 25), Jay Wilson (December 6) and Steve Keiser (January 25) and Lura Groen (July 26). Rebecca also has a stole on display with the "For All Saints" Stoles Project of the Lutheran Network for Inclusive Vision, which she started to present to the Churchwide Assembly in Denver (August 1999).

November: Death of Sister Bernedetta- 1591-1661; Benedetta Carlini was a Catholic mystic and lesbian nun, who lived in Counter-Reformation Italy during the sixteenth and seventeenth century. Sister Bernedetta Carlini made love to Sister Bartholomea taking on the appearance of Jesus or a beautiful adolescent boy with a deepened voice.

November 1997: Pastor Jane L. Stwart quietly resigns from the ELCA's Southeastern Iowa Synod to avoid disciplinary action- Jane was ordained in May of 1985, after being aware of God's call to ministry of Word and Sacrament since 1972 when Jane was 15. Jane has a stole on display with the "For All Saints" Stoles Project of the Lutheran Network for Inclusive Vision.

November 1: All Saints Day- This is a good day to remember all of the queer saints/sinners who have served the church throughout the ages (known and unknown.) You can remember the unkown by reading the story of Pastor X (published in the Gay Lutheran Sept.-Oct 1974) and Pastor D (published in the Gay Lutheran Jan. 1975).[202] Here are a few more individuals that have names, but no dates connected to them:

- Pat Sample and Lynn Griffis "whose call to ordained ministries was denied by the ELCA's predecessor-Church denominations";
- Pr John L. Ames who was ordained in 1989;
- Pastor J. Thomas George, who continues "to do ministry without my collar!";
- Pastor Ruth Bruland, formerly a pastor in the Grand Canyon Synod of the ELCA;
- Pastor Bill Stark was known for his love of high church rituals. "Bill wanted nothing more than to serve his church and his God but he found the restrictions of the church placed on him as a gay man impossible to abide by. In time Bill left his congregation, and finally, the ministry." Bill was killed shortly after moving to Texas to become a parole officer, and his murder has not been solved.

The above mentioned have stoles are on display with the "For All Saints" Stoles Project of the Lutheran Network for Inclusive Vision.

---

[202] The Gay Lutheran is archived at: www.meganrohrer.com/archive

November 3, 1998: Pastor John Carrier retires his stoles- On Reformation Day, John retired his liturgically colored stoles and vowed to only where a rainbow stole whenever he vests "until the Church's policies have changed to include queer clergy who live in blessed union with a life partner." A white wedding stole given to John as an ordination gift in 1985 is on display with the "For All Saints" Stoles Project of the Lutheran Network for Inclusive Vision and is signed by others who supported his stance.

November 4, 1995: Ordination of Pastor Kelli Shepard: Kelli is a member of the Extraordinary Lutheran Ministries roster who is currently working as a Chaplain Coordinator and ACPE Associate Supervisor at the Banner Good Samaritan Medical Center in Phoenix, Arizona. Pastor Kelli received a Bachelor of Social Work from Capital University in Columbus, Ohio and went on to receive her Master of Divinity from Trinity Lutheran Seminary, also in Columbus. In 1995, she was ordained in the Evangelical Lutheran Church in America and went on to serve as pastor of an ELCA congregation in metro Chicago. Kelli came to Good Samaritan in 1997 and successfully completed a year-long CPE residency. She continued her CPE journey as a Supervisory student and was certified as an Associate Supervisor in April 2003. Kelli enjoys the outdoors by camping and hiking and can regularly be found at America West Arena cheering on the Phoenix Mercury.

November 7, 1999: Installation of Pastor Jeff Johnson at University Lutheran Chapel: Pastor Jeff was installed as pastor of University Lutheran Chapel and the Lutheran campus pastor at the University of California, Berkeley, on November 7, 1999. Prior to this call to the Chapel, Jeff served as pastor of First United Lutheran Church in San Francisco's Richmond District since his ordination on January 20, 1990 (see January).

Jeff is a 1984 graduate of California Lutheran University where he received degrees in German and History. In 1988, he received a Master of Divinity degree from Pacific Lutheran Theological Seminary in Berkeley. Upon graduation, he worked as Director of AIDS Education for Lutheran Social Services of Northern California, where he coordinated the first national ELCA Bishops

Convocation on HIV and authored a curriculum series used by northern California Lutheran congregations responding to the HIV epidemic.

In 1990, he founded Lutheran Lesbian and Gay Ministry with his colleagues, pastors Ruth Frost and Phyllis Zillhart, to provide an outreach to the lesbian, gay, bisexual and transgendered community of the San Francisco Bay Area. These three were the first openly lesbian and gay people to be ordained in the Lutheran Church.

Pastor Johnson was ordained extraordinarily (January 20) with a call from First United Lutheran Church (San Francisco). As a result First United was expelled from the ELCA in 1995 for calling him to be their pastor. University Lutheran Chapel has been censured for having called Jeff in November 1999.

Jeff has served two terms as Dean of the ELCA's San Francisco Conference of Lutheran Churches; is a member of the Steering Committee for Religious Witness with Homeless People; is a founder and past president of the Extraordinary Candidacy Project; is the immediate past chair of the Homelessness Task Force for the Telegraph Area Association; is co-chair of the University Religious Council at CAL Berkeley; was co-chair with Jeannine Jansson of GoodSoil in Orlando; is on the Steering Committe for the Interfaith Committee for Worker Justice; and is an Internship Supervisor and Teaching Parish Supervisor for Pacific Lutheran Theological Seminary. He lives in Oakland's Piedmont District in a 1928 stucco bungalow. He enjoys a good mystery novel, gardening in his back yard, fishing, home-repair, relaxing in coffee-shops, walking by the Bay, and spending time with his partner, friends, and family.

November 9: Feast day of St. Matrona/Babylas of Perge (According to the Orthodox Calendar)- Matrona/Babylas was a female born ascetic who wore male monastic habits. Matrona, fleeing a bad husband, assumed male garb and the name of Babylus and entered a monastery. However zir identity was discovered and zie entered a convent at Emesa where zie became abbess until zie was forced to flee zir husband again. Matrona/Babylas hid herself in a ruined heathen temple at Berytus and lived the life of a recluse until the death of zir husband.

November 11, 2001: Pastor Arlo Peterson Installed at Holy Trinity Lutheran Church: (See September 22) this work."

November 17, 2007: Ordination of Pastor Jen Rude at Resurrection Lutheran Church, Chicago: Pastor Jen is a member of the Extraordinary Lutheran Ministries roster, a graduate of Augustana College in Sioux Falls, South Dakota and received her MDiv from the Pacific School of Religion in Berkeley, California. Pastor Jen Rude currently serves as the Community Minister at Resurrection Lutheran Church, an ELCA congregation in Chicago and as a Youth Outreach Minister with homeless and runaway youth in Chicago at The Night Ministry.

Jen was a candidate in both the ELCA and ELM candidacy process. Her Sierra Pacific Synod ELCA approval committee met in October 2006. Although her small panel recommended approval, the larger full committee decided to make no decision.

November 18, 1986: Ordination of Pastor Richard Andersen at Luther Seminary in St. Paul, Minnesota- Pastor Richard is a member of the Extraordinary Lutheran Ministries roster.

November 18, 2006: Ordination of Pastor Megan Rohrer at HerChurch (Ebenezer) Lutheran Church, San Francisco- Author of this book and member of the Extraordinary Lutheran Ministries roster, Pastor Megan is a graduate of Augustana College in Sioux Falls, South Dakota, received and MDiv from the Pacific School of Religion in Berkeley, California. Megan was called by four Lutheran congregations (HerChurch, Christ, St. Francis and Sts. Mary and Martha) to serve as the director of the Welcome Ministry serving the homeless and hungry in San Francisco. In addition to being the first seminarian to become rostered with the Extraordinary Lutheran Ministries as a matter of conscience (without ever being rejected by the ELCA), Megan is also the first openly transgender pastor ordained in the Lutheran church in the United States.

November 23, 1986: Ordination of Pastor Rebecca J. Hostetler. (see October 31)

November 29, 1995: Death of Joel Workin- An exceptionally gifted young Lutheran seminarian whose call to ministry and passion for proclaiming the gospel of Jesus Christ were tragically pre-empted by the discriminatory policies of the ELCA and his untimely death from AIDS. Joel was one of the Berkeley three that came out at Pacific Lutheran Theological Seminary. Extraordinary Lutheran Ministries' Joel Raydon Workin Memorial Scholarship Fund was first established in 1995 through the generosity of Joel's family, colleagues and closest friends.

December 1: World AIDS Day- While there there are many saints that we can pray for this day, here are a few to include: Joel Workin; Pastor Phil Knutson; and...

- Pastor Rollie Severson died of AIDS related causes in 1989, while serving as Campus Pastor at the University of Miami, Coral Gables, Florida. Rollie spent his life as a Lutheran pastor afraid of being 'discovered.' Prior to serving in Miami he was campus pastor at the University of Minnesota. On the AIDS quilt memorial, Rollie is remembered with his Jewish partner John Paul Fetterman. Rollie has a stole on display with the "For All Saints" Stoles Project of the Lutheran Network for Inclusive Vision and is signed by others who supported his stance.
- Pastor Domas Planas Befort died of AIDS and has a stole on display with the "For All Saints" Stoles Project of the Lutheran Network for Inclusive Vision.

December 4: Feast day of Saint Barbara (According to the Orthodox Calendar)- d.c.300 CE; was an Amazonian Catholic saint who rebelled against her pagan father's wish for zir to marry by rejecting all suitors, converting to Christianity and converting a bath house into a church. Legend has it that Barbara's father retaliated by dragging zir to a mountain top and killing zir, only to be killed by lightening as he climbed down the mountain. Barbara is celebrated as a gender variant or transgender macho male saint who is able to control lightening.

December 6: Ordination of Pastor Jay Wilson in San Francisco, California: Pastor Jay is a member of the Extraordinary Lutheran Ministries roster who was called by First United Lutheran in San Francisco to serve as Assistant Director of the Welcome Ministry in San Francisco to the homeless and hungry. Jay completed his Masters in Social Work from College of St. Catherine/St. Thomas University and just completed his Masters in Divinity from Luther Seminary in St. Paul, Minnesota. While attending Luther Seminary, he co-founded AGAPE, a group for LGBTQ students and allies, and transitioned female-to-male in appearance while living on campus. After being removed from the process to become a pastor in the ELCA due to gender identity and sexual orientation.

December 14: Feast day of St. Venantius Fortunatus, bishop (According to the Old Roman Calendar)- c.530-c.603; Venantius Fortunatus was a poet, born c. 530 in Treviso, near Ravenna in Italy. He spent his time as court poet to the Merovingians and is considered a spiritual ancestor of same-sex lovers. After visiting the tomb of St. Martin of tours at St. Hilary at Poitiers, he decided to enter a monastery. He continued to write poetry, some of which have a permanent place in Catholic hymnody, for instance the Easter season hymns Vexilla Regis and the Pange Lingua (Sing, O my tongue, of the battle). Before he died he was made bishop of Poitiers.

December 14: Feast day of St. John of the Cross, priest and doctor (according to the Church of England and the New Roman Calendar)- 1542-1591; St. John of Cross was one of the great Spanish mystics, whose outstanding Dark Night of the Soul is still read by all interested in Catholic mysticism. St. John, like other mystics such as St. Theresa of Avila, used the language of courtly love to describe his relationship with Christ. He also discussed, with rare candor, the sexual stimulation of prayer, and the fact that mystics experience sexual arousal during prayer. With the male Christ of course, this amounts to a homoeroticism in prayer. He was beatified by Clement X in 1675, canonized by Benedict XIII in 1726, and declared a Doctor of Church Universal by Pius XI in 1926.

December 16: Birthday of Pastor Ruth Frost: Formerly a teacher and drug and alcohol counselor; Ruth was ordained on January 20, 1990 and served as the Associate Pastor for Outreach and Evangelism at St. Francis Lutheran Church, San Francisco.

In 1990, she founded Lutheran Lesbian and Gay Ministry along with his colleagues, Pastors Jeff Johnson and Phyllis Zillhart, to provide an outreach to the lesbian, gay, bisexual and transgendered community of the San Francisco Bay Area. These three persons were the first openly lesbian and gay people to be ordained in the Lutheran Church. (see January 20)

Ruth is an accomplished stained glass artist who has completed projects at St. Francis and Lutheran Church of Our Redeemer in Sacramento, CA.

December 17: The Three Young Men (According to the Orthodox Calendar; they are sometimes remembered with Daniel on the 18th of December)- Daniel and the three young men would have been taken to Babylon as court eunuchs. Eunuchs are by far the most discussed sexual minorities in both the Hebrew and Greek bibles. It is interesting to note that while eunuchs were excluded from the community of Israel by Deuteronomy, Isaiah 56:1-8 and Wisdom 3:13-14 both specifically include them in God's blessing. Isaiah rejects the provision of the law which rejects the eunuch and expands the definition of God's people beyond the patriarchal family that is characterized the early history of Israel.

December 20th: Ruth and Naomi (According to the Orthodox Calendar)- c1100 BCE; Ruth was the great-grandmother of King David, and is a direct ancestor of Jesus. Although Deuteronomy 23:3 specifically states that no Moabite is to be admitted to the assembly of the Lord (a position vigorously pursued later by such nationalists as Ezra and Nehemiah [Ezra:1,2,12; 103,18,44, Neh 13:23, 25, 27-28, 30]), Ruth was a Moabite women.

The focus of the story is on her loving relationship with Naomi. At Naomi's suggestion, Ruth marries a kinsman of Naomi, called Boaz, in order to perpetuate her dead husband Mahlon's line (Ruth 4:12-14, 17). Though questions remain about the intention Ruth 1:16-18, it is still one of the most frequently used texts at opposite-sex marriage ceremonies: "for whither thou goest, I will go; and where thou lodgest, I will lodge: thy people shall be my people, and thy God my God: Where thou diest, will I die, and there will I be buried: the LORD do so to me, and more also, if ought but death part thee and me."

December 24: Feast day of St. Eugenia/Eugenios of Alexandria (According to the Orthodox Calendar)- Eugenia/Eugenios was a female born ascetic who wore male monastic habits. Eugenia/Eugenios entered a monastery and remained living the life of a humble monk until elected abbot. Zie continued to live in a cell that was built in next to the monestary while abbot.

December 24: Feast day of SS. Protus and Hyacinth, martyrs (According to the Orthodox Calendar)- Eunuchs and companions of St. Eugenia of Alexandria, they were two of her teachers who accompanied her on a somewhat romantic journey, and at the end were martyred with her.

December 27: Feast Day of St. John the Evangelist (According to all Western Calendars)- 1st Century CE; The love between Christ and St. John (the beloved disciple) has been seen as homoerotic for centuries. Of particular note in the Gospel of John (13:21-30) is the twice mentioned position of the beloved reclining next to Jesus and Simon's acknowledgement that Jesus will tell the beloved information that he will not share with the rest of the disciples. The Gospel of John also sets up a scene at the crucifixion (19:26-27) that is parallel to a Jewish wedding ceremony: "When Jesus saw his mother and the disciple whom he loved standing beside her, he said to his mother, 'Woman, here is your son.' Then he said to the disciple, 'Here is your mother.' And from that hour the disciple took her into his own home."[203]

December 29: Day for remembering David the Prophet (According to the Old Roman Calendar)- 1035?-960?BCE; David and Jonathon pledge to love each other more then they love women (for David this would mean his more than 700 wives and 300 concubines). Scholars have argued that Saul's rage against David was jealously that he loved his son more than he loved Saul. Queer theologians continue to argue that David goes on to become the lover of YHVH who is the Top of All Tops.

December 31, 1995: Festival of the Expulsion: St. Francis and First United (see January)

---

[203] See Jennings Jr, Theodore W., The Man Jesus Loved: Homoerotic Narratives From the New Testament, Pilgrim Press, 2003.

History's Many Names for Queer Spiritual Leaders

History will show how much credence should be given to this statement. But there are other signs, no less sure than oracles, which threaten a change in the monastic regime.[204]
—Apology of the Augusburg Confession

This book has focused on the ways that the ancient understandings and tradition of the Lutheran church are queer. At the edges of this is the witness of faith communities throughout the world who have also celebrated the spirituality of queer individuals because of, not in spite of their queer in sexuality and gender. Below I have outlined some of the many ancient names for these queer spiritual leaders.[205] It is my hope that this list will challenge those who falsely claim that queer gender and sexuality are renounced in all major religions and in other parts of the country. The real truth is that contemporary Christians have erased the longer history and only have ears to hear the voices that agree with them. If you are interested in learning more about the fringe group of stoic Christian missionaries who spread homophobia across the globe through colonialism, read Byrne Fone's, <u>Homophobia: A History</u>. If you do not have the time to read the 421 page book, thinking about the ways contemporary conservative Christians have dominated the current political landscape on issues will give you an idea of how a fringe group can use fear to perpetuate their own power and agenda.

---

[204] Article XXVII: art. i, par. 13, par. 4

[205] Primary resources from this section include: Roscoe, Will, <u>Third Sex, Third Gender: Beyond Sexual Dimorphism in Culture and History</u>, Ed. Herdt, Gilbert, Zone Books, 1994; <u>Omingender;</u> and <u>Cassell's Encyclopedia.</u>

Native American/American Indian Queer Spiritual Leaders

Tribe	Term		Healers?	
Achomawi	MTF:	(men-women)	Yes	M/F
Acoma	MTF:	Mujerado ("womaned") Qo-Qoy-Mo (Effeminate person) Kokwina (Men-women)		
Aleut	MTF:	Shupan		
Arapaho	MTF:	Haxu'xan		
Assiniboine	MTF:	Win'yan inkwenu'ze Winktan		
Atsugewi	MTF:	Yaawa	Yes	M
	FTM:	Brumaiwi		
Bankalachi	MTF:		No	M
Bella Coola	MTF:	Sx'ints		
Chumash	MTF:		No	M
Chetco River	MTF:		Yes	F
Cheyenne	MTF:	Heemaneh'	Yes	M
Cocopa	MTF:	Elha		
	FTM:	Warrhameh		
Coeur d'Alène	FTM:	St'amia (hermaphrodite)		
Cree	MTF:	Aayahkwew	Yes	M/F
Crow	MTF:	Bate		
	FTM:	(woman chief)		
Chugach-Eskimo	MTF:	Aranu'tiq		
Dakota (Santee)	MTF:	Winkta		
Diagueño	MTF:		No	M
Eskimo (Chugash)	MTF:		No	M/F
Eskimo (St.	MTF:	Anasik	Yes	M/F

Lawrence)				
	FTM:	Uktasik		
Eskimo (Inuit)	MTF:	Angakkuq, Angakok or Angaqoq	Yes	
Eyak	MTF:	(No good)		
Flathead	MTF:	Ma'Kali, me'mi, tcin-mamalks (Dress as a woman)	Yes	M/F
Gabrielino	MTF:		No	M
Hidatsa	MTF:	Miati (To be impelled against one's will to act the woman) Biatti	Yes	M
Hopi	MTF:	Na'dle (being transformed)		
	FTM:	Nadle		
Houma	FTM:	Femme chef (?)		
Huchnom	MTF:	Iwap kuti		
Ingalik	MTF:	(woman pretender)		
	FTM:	(men pretenders)		
Isleta	MTF:	Lhunide		
Juaneño	MTF:	Kwit		
Kaniagmiut	MTF:	Shupan (?)		
Kaska	FTM:	(Females in a man's role, woman chief)		
Kato	MTF:		No	M
Kawaiisu	MTF:		No	M
Kitanemuk	MTF:		No	M
Klamath	MTF:	Tw!inna'ek	Yes	M
	FTM:	Tw!inna'ek		
Kutenai	MTF:	Tupatke'tek (to imitate a woman)		

	FTM:	(manlike woman)		
Kwakiutl	MTF:	(Act like a woman)		
Laguna	MTF:	Mujerado (Man-woman ?) Kokwimu, kokwe'ma		
Lakota (Ogala)	MTF:	Winkte (Desirous of being women, would-be woman or hermaphrodite)		
Lakota (Teton)	MTF:		Yes	M
Lakota	FTM:	Koskalaka "lesbian" or "double woman's daughters" (wiya numpa)		
Lassik	MTF:	Murfidai ("Hermaphrodite")	No	M/F
Luiseño	MTF:	Cuit Cuut		
Maidu	Both:	Suku	Yes	M
Mandan	MTF:	Mihdäckä (Mih-hä = woman) Mihdacke		
Maricopa	MTF:	Ilyaxi' (impolite) Yesa'an (polite - barren man or woman) A vial y xa' (mountain person)	No	M
	FTM:	Kwiraxame		
Mattole	MTF:		Yes	F
Miami	MTF:	Waupeengwoatar (The White Face)		
Miwok	MTF:	Osabu (Osa = woman)		
Modoc	MTF:		Yes	M/F
Mohave	MTF:	Alyha (Coward?)	Yes	M/F
	FTM:	Hwame	Yes	

136

		Hwami		
Mono	MTF:	Tai'up	No	M
Natchez	MTF:	(Chef des femmes)		
Navajo (Navaho)	MTF:	Nadle, Nadleehe, Nadleehi or Nadleh "Being transformed" or "one who is constantly changing" Tsilth-'tsa-assun "man and woman"	Yes	M
	FTM:	Nadle		
Nomlaki	MTF:	Walusa, tohket (Hermaphrodite, "boy who goes around the them women all the time)		
Ojibwa	MTF:	Agokwa (man-woman or split testicles)		
Omaha	MTF: FTM:	Mixu'ga (Instructed by the moon) Minquga (trans or third gender)	Yes	M/ F
Oto	MTF:	Mixo'ge		
Paiute, Northern	MTF:	Tübas, t'üBáse, moyo'ne, tüBázanàna (polite) Düba's (sterile person)	No	M/F
	FTM:	Düba's Moroni noho Tüvasa		
Paiute, Southern	MTF:	Tüwasawuts, maipots, onobakö, töwahawöts, Maai'pots	No	M
Panamint			No	M
Patwin	MTF:	Panaro bobum pi (He has two (sexes))		
Piegan	MTF:	Ake'skassi (acts like a woman)	Yes	M

	FTM:	(manly-hearted woman, female 'berdache')		
Pima	MTF:	Wik'ovat (like a girl)		
Pomo, Northern	MTF:	Das (Da = woman)	No	M/F
Pomo, Southern	MTF:	T!un	No	M/F
Ponca	MTF:	Misu'ga Morphodite (hermaphrodite)		
Potawatomi	MTF:	M'netokwe (Manito plus female suffix)		
Quinault	MTF:	Keknatsa'nxwixw (part woman)		
	FTM:	(man-acting)		
Salinan	MTF:	Joyas (Spanish: gem, jewel)	No	M
Sauk	MTF:	I-coo-coo-a		
Shasta	MTF:	Gitukuwaki	No	F
Shoshoni (Lemhi)	MTF:	Tübasa (sterile) tenanduakia (tenap = man)		
	FTM:	Tübasa tenanduakia waip:ü sunwe (woman half?)		
Shoshoni (Bannock)	MTF:	Tuva'sa (Vasap = dry)		
Shoshoni (Promontory Point)	MTF:	Tubasa waip (waip = woman)		
Shoshoni (Gosiute)	MTF:	Tuvasa		
Shoshoni (Nevada)	MTF:	Tuyayap Tubasa'a (half man, half woman) Tangwu waip (man-woman)	No	M

		Tangowaip (man-woman) Waip: sinwa (half woman)		
	FTM:	Nüwüdüka (female hunter) tangowaip tangowaipü		
Tewa	MTF:	Kwido Kweedo Kwidõ Kossa Kwirana		
Tillamook	MTF:		Yes	F
Tlingit	MTF:	Gatxan (Coward)		
Tolowa	MTF:		Yes	F
Tsimshian		Pestilence		
Tübatulabal	MTF:	Huiy	No	M
Ute (Southern)	MTF:	Tuwasawits Tuwasawuts	No	M/F
Wailaki	MTF:	Clele		
Winnebago	MTF:	Shiánge (Eunuch, unmanly man)		
Wintu	MTF:		No	M/F
Wishram	MTF:	Ikte'laskait	No	M/F
Wiyot	MTF:		Yes	F
Yana	MTF:	Lo'ya	No	M
Yokuts (Kocheyali)	MTF:	Tonoo'tcim ("undertaker")		
Yokuts (Paleuyami)	MTF:	Tono'cim		
Yokuts (Tachi)	MTF:	Tonochim Lokowitnono	No	M
Yokuts	MTF:	Tono'cim	No	M

(Michahai)				
Yokuts (Yaudanchi)	MTF:	Tongochim	No	M
Yokuts (Wakasachi)	MTF:	Tai'yap	No	M
Yuki	MTF:	I-wa-musp (man-woman) Iwap-naip (man-girl) Iwop-naiip (men-girls)	No	M/F
	FTM:	Musp-iwap naip		
Yuma	MTF:	Elxa	No	M/F
	FTM:	Kwe'rhame (Kwiraxame)		
Yurok	MTF:	Wegern	Yes	F
Zuni	MTF:	Kokk'okshi (or Kokkokwe) "Raw People" Ko'thlama Koyemshi Lha'mana	Yes	
	FTM:	Katsotse or Katsosi'		

Latin and South American Queer Spiritual Leaders

Tribe/People		Term	Healers?
Kechki of Guatemala	MTF	Ishquicuink "sometimes acts like a man, sometimes acts like a woman"	Yes
Lache	MTF	Cusmos	
Hatian	Lesbian	Madivinez (Zami)	Yes
Manta of Ecuador	Gender Queer	Hierodules	Yes
Mayans of Mexico and	Transgender		Yes

Guatemala				
Gran Chaco of Paraguay	MTF	Mbaya	Yes	
Moche of Peru	Homoerotic		Yes	
Trujilo of Peru	Gender Queer		Yes	
Mexico	Lesbian	Patlache Mocihuapoitiani Tepixuia		
Columbia, Venezuela and Brazil	Homoerotic, sometimes Gender Queer	Piache	Yes	
Jamaican	Homoerotic	Pukkumina (or Pocomania)	Yes	
Puna of Ecuador	Homoerotic			
Aztec	MTF	Tezcatlipoca		

African Queer Spiritual Leaders

Tribe/People		Term	Healers?	
Lugbara	FTM:	Agule "like men"	Yes	
Egypt	MTF:	Al-Jink or El-Gink[eyn] Gallos (bakoloi, bakides, kybebes, metragyrtes and metrizantes)	Yes	
Ngaju Dayak of Borneo	MTF	Basir	Yes	
Maguzawa of Nigeria	MTF	Yan Daudu Yan Hamsin		

Big Nambas of Vanuatu		Dubut	Yes
Zulu	Gender Queer	Isangoma (pl. Izangoma, or Sangom)	Yes
Mesopotamia	MTF	Kalaturru Kalum Kulu'u Kurgarru (kurgarra) "neither male nor female" Pilpili Sinnishanu "woman-like one"	Yes
Kalui of Papa New Guinea	Homoer otic	Keraki Kiwai	Yes
Ambo of Angola	MTF	Kimbanda	Yes
Libya	Gender Queer	Machlyes	
Iban Dayak of Borneo	MTF	Manang Bali	Yes

Asian Queer Spiritual Leaders

Tribe/People		Term	Healers?	
Idus Valley Civilization, India	Homoer otic	A-Jami, Jami	Yes	
Libyan	FTM	Amazon	Yes	
Philippines	Gender Queer, MTF	Bayoguin	Yes	
Hindu	MTF	Bhaki Napunsaka "nonmale"	No	

	Third Gender	Trititya Prakriti "third nature"		
Ancient China	Male Eunuchs		Yes	
	Gender Queer	Shih-Niang "master girl"	Yes	
	FTM	Shih Fu "stone maiden"		
	MTF	Shih Nan "stone man"		
Uruk	MTF	Assinnu	Yes	
India	MTF	Hijra Khoja	Yes	
Korea	Homoerotic: MTF	Hwarang "flower boys of Silla" Paksu Mudang	Yes	
Thailand	MTF	Kathoey		
Aphaca or Lebanon		Kelah (pl. Kelabim)		
Turkish	MTF	Kocek	Yes	
Siberian Kamchadal (Itelmensy)	MTF	Koe'kcuc	Yes	
Aleuts of NE Siberia	FTM	Qa'cikicheca (appareled like a man)	Yes	
Arabic	MTF	Mukhannath (pl Mukhannathun)	Yes	
Naas, Naassenes and Ophites of Israel				
Canannite or Ugaritic	MTF	Qadesh (pl Qedeshim) "holy ones"	Yes	
Chukchi of North Asia	MTF	"soft man"	Yes	
Japan	MTF	Wikiga-Winagu (become female in services called	Yes	

		winagu nati)		
Southern Tungras people from the Gold (Nanai) Tribe (current boarder of China and Russia)	Sometimes homoerotic	Ayami	Yes	

European Queer Spiritual Leaders

Tribe/People/ Land	Term		Healers?	
Ancient Greece	FTM	Amazon	Yes	
	Homoerotic Eunuchs	Semnotatoi		
Toradja Bare's (Celebes)	MTF	Bajasa	Yes	
Thracian/Greco-Roman	MTF	Baptai "Baptists"	Yes	
Greco-Roman		Megabyzos (pl. Megabyzoi)	Yes	
Cathars of Southern France	Homoerotic	Bougres "buggers"		
Island of Cos	MTF	"Brides"	Yes	
Germany	Gender Queer	Tuisto "dual being"		

Made in the USA
Columbia, SC
08 March 2022